About the Author

Publius was the pen name used by James Madison, Alexander Hamilton and John Jay in The Federalist Papers. The name Publius was chosen because Publius Valerius was one of the founders of the Roman Republic. Since Madison, Hamilton, Jay and others were founding a new republic and NOT a democracy here in the United States, they used the name of the founder of the Roman Republic to promote the Constitutional Republic they gave us. This historical fact is the reason I chose the pen name Madame Publius to educate my readers about the Constitutional Republic created by the U.S. Constitution.

The U.S. Paper Dollar

Madame Publius

The U.S. Paper Dollar

Olympia Publishers
London

www.olympiapublishers.com
OLYMPIA PAPERBACK EDITION

Copyright © Madame Publius 2024

The right of Madame Publius to be identified as author of
this work has been asserted in accordance with sections 77 and 78 of
the Copyright, Designs and Patents Act 1988.

All Rights Reserved

No reproduction, copy or transmission of this publication
may be made without written permission.
No paragraph of this publication may be reproduced,
copied or transmitted save with the written permission of the publisher,
or in accordance with the provisions
of the Copyright Act 1956 (as amended).

Any person who commits any unauthorised act in relation to
this publication may be liable to criminal
prosecution and civil claims for damage.

A CIP catalogue record for this title is
available from the British Library.

ISBN: 978-1-80439-784-8

The opinions expressed in this book are the author's own and do not
reflect the views of the publisher, author's employer, organisation,
committee or other group or individual.

First Published in 2024

Olympia Publishers
Tallis House
2 Tallis Street
London
EC4Y 0AB

Printed in Great Britain

Dedication

This book is dedicated to the unfailing, singular and inspirational memories of the Framers.

Acknowledgments

This book was only possible because of the efforts taken by the Framers to preserve their writings.

"Here is wisdom, let him that hath understanding count the number of the beast: for it is the number of a man; and his number is Six hundred threescore and six." (Rev. 13:18) (emphasis added)

John the Revelator,
Revelation (13:18)

"... his number is Six hundred threescore and six."
John the Revelator,
Revelation (13:18)

Foreword

In June of 2019, I submitted my manuscript, *Spectacles of Turbulence and Contention: Unmasking "our democracy" and the "rule of law" with The Federalist Papers* (hereinafter **Spectacles**), to several publishers. None of the traditional publishers even responded to my submission. I then submitted my manuscript to the self-publishing market but was unable to use their services as the required payment to publish my manuscript was too high. I was in severe financial distress at the time and unable to pay their fees so my manuscript went unpublished.

Using the words of Madison, Hamilton and Jay from The Federalist Papers, my manuscript highlighted how far we have strayed from the Republic that the Framers designed for us in the U.S. Constitution. In addition to highlighting the differences between republics and democracies and our descent into the "turbulence and contention" of democracy, I also wrote **Spectacles** as a warning. In **Spectacles**, I correctly predicted some of the catastrophes coming to our nation as a result of our apostasy from the sacred law given to us in the U.S. Constitution and our moral decline as a country.

Specifically, I predicted, among other things, that the U.S. would be hit with a biological attack and as I predicted, a biological weapon, also known as the Coronavirus or COVID-19, hit the U.S. in January of 2020. I predicted that the attack would happen within five years from the date of my submission on June 23, 2019, but it took less than one year for my prediction to materialize. I also predicted that the attack would come from China or Russia. It did. I also predicted that it would hit either New York or LA first. New York was considered the epicenter of the outbreak. I also predicted that large, traitorous American corporations would try and fashion a narrative to deny that China was involved, but, after a long time, this narrative would fail. As I predicted, we heard the narrative from the media, the tech giants and others that China was not involved. Finally, just as I predicted, we are beginning to see the proverbial dam break in this regard as revelations are coming out proving that the biological attack came from Wuhan, China and not from nature as the propagandists claimed.

In my second book, **Hypocritical Nation**, that I wrote in 2020, I predicted that the U.S. would face a Chinese invasion by 2025 following a series of cyber-attacks, an EMP and other subversive maneuvers that would be designed to take out our electrical grid and our infrastructure before the invasion. The resulting pandemonium I predicted would set up a "Trojan Horse" invasion that would begin in Hawaii and then continue on through to the West Coast and onto the East under the guise of an UN Blue Helmet humanitarian mission that the CCP would be orchestrating.

As with **Spectacles**, when no one in the media was even talking about pandemics, no one was talking about a war with China when I wrote **Hypocritical Nation**. Now, war with China is being talked about everywhere and the Chinese balloon highlighted the fact that EMPs are considered to be a real threat. We are also seeing our infrastructure being systematically destroyed with over one hundred food plants being destroyed and burnt to the ground in just the past year. Commercial egg laying chicken farms have also been attacked and destroyed killing millions of hens. Supply chains have been disrupted. Energy prices have skyrocketed as our energy industry is being targeted as well. These are not random events, but part of the CCP's unrestricted war effort being waged against the U.S. just as I predicted in *Hypocritical Nation*. Unfortunately, my efforts at publication for my second book ended just like it did with *Spectacles*.

This book raises the alarm once again regarding our nation. Trying to protect ourselves from our history has only served to destroy our ability to see. This book presents a piece of our history that has been changed, buried and distorted. This destructive work was deliberate. Our leaders and their accomplices changed history in order to turn our Christian-centered, Constitutional Republic into a destructive, democratic-hybrid based war machine. I will mention that defensive posturing is not in my future. I'm not interested in any "holes" with my premise. If someone has a better explanation for the history that I present here, then, they should make their case. Otherwise, everything else is simply meant to be a distraction from the truth.

Madame Publius

Chapter 1
The Mark of the Beast

"Mr. Read, thought the words, if not struck out, would be as alarming as *the mark of the Beast in Revelations*." Id. (emphasis added)

Delegate George Read,
James Madison's Notes of the Constitutional Convention, August 16, 1787.

The Bible teaches us that "the love of money is the root of all evil." (1 Tim. 6:10) Now, I know that this scripture is often taken out of context. People sometimes argue that money itself is the root of all evil, but that is not what the scripture says. It clearly states that the **LOVE** of money is the root cause; so, in case you missed it, let me repeat myself – Paul said that ALL evil, not just some of it, but ALL evil has its root in the *love of money*. When taken literally, this means that every, single act of evil committed throughout the world can be traced back to one thing – the *love of money*. This is profound.

We should ask ourselves – what is it about money that entices us as humans to love it so much that we end up turning ourselves over to evil? This work delves into that question by examining the history of money in the United States. Understanding money and how it operates is imperative for anyone who wants to take precautions against any unnecessary enhancements that elevate the love of money in their lives. Our ignorance and complacency in these matters has brought us to a great crisis of which few, if any, are aware.

Much of our country's history has been under attack with schemes like the 1619 Project and the traitorous attempts to erase names and monuments from our buildings and landscape. When we lose our past, we lose understanding. We have no point of reference to even grasp what we are missing. The overwhelming majority in the U.S. knows little to nothing about our Founding Constitutional past, and it has had an overwhelming negative impact on our everyday lives. When correctly understood, we are better able to remove the love of money from our lives. If such things had only been taught and correctly understood, we would have had fewer wars and far less crime and tragedy.

Let's go back to the beginning of our monetary history, when some of our Founding Fathers tried to warn us about the dangers of a love for paper money. It took place on a hot summer's day in Philadelphia on August 16, 1787. This important event was one of many debates that took place during our Constitutional Convention that year. This particular debate centered on the question of whether or not the phrase to "emit bills of credit on the credit of the US" should be inserted into the Constitution.

While it might appear somewhat innocuous at first glance or even too legalistic, the phrase had horrible implications on our society. According to the record, if the phrase had been inserted into the Constitution, it would have given power to the Congress to issue paper money. Following the debate on the matter, a vote was taken and the language was rejected and, therefore, kept out of the Constitution. Now, of course, some of you are thinking to yourselves, *But I thought that paper money was already legal tender in the United States today?* The better question you should be asking is, "If the authorization had never been inserted into the Constitution by Amendment or otherwise, then how was it possible that Congress was able to authorize the printing of paper money?" This book answers that question, but first we need to finish our discussion on that important debate of August 16, 1787.

Although most of what happened during the Constitutional Convention has been lost to history for one reason or another, James Madison kept personal notes of the proceedings. He was very meticulous in his note-keeping and thankfully those notes were preserved and eventually published. Granted, it is a tome, but it is rich in Constitutional detail and history. Fortunately, Madison's record also includes the debate that took place surrounding the paper money issue.

Now, initially, you might be tempted to yawn, or you might even be thinking that this discussion is much ado about nothing since paper money is a foregone conclusion and has been in use for over one hundred and fifty-two years. Ignorance is, as they say, bliss. This is especially true with the average U.S. citizen who has an attention span that can barely last longer than one hundred and twenty characters or a thirty-second video clip, so please, try and fight the temptation to yawn. Try and imagine yourself as one of the very few conscientiously curious seekers of Constitutional truth, and then get ready, because it is going to be a bit of a wild ride from hereon out.

During the debate, one particular Delegate to the Convention argued vehemently against inserting the proposed language. Apparently, he saw ramifications to this power going well beyond the printing presses. He saw it as a dangerous precipice from which we would fall as a nation. Apparently, this Delegate also saw that the inclusion of the language would fulfill a specific prophecy found in the Book of Revelation. The Delegate's name was George Read.

Delegate Read was an attorney. He was also one of the signers of the Declaration of Independence, which means that he was one of only fifty-six individuals in all of history to make such a commitment to this country. He also represented the State of Delaware as a delegate to the 1787 U.S. Constitutional Convention, which was the situs of our debate. It was in his capacity as Delaware's Delegate to the Convention, wherein he makes a startling claim. As mentioned previously, the debate centered on whether or not Congress should be given the power to print paper money. Delegate Read stood up to argue against authorization saying that such a power would portend to darker things. The following entry can be found in Madison's Notes from the Convention:

"Mr. Read, thought the words, if not struck out, would be as **alarming as the mark of the Beast in Revelations**." Constitutional Convention, August 16, 1787. (emphasis added)

This entry, as far as I can tell, has never been referenced nor analyzed for its meaning in any other historical work. His comment is significant, however, given his stature and reputation and the consensus that the Convention eventually came to on the subject of paper money. As such, his comment should alarm us and invite serious analysis. Clearly, Delegate Read was not given to trivial pursuits. He was an educated Patriot who had put everything on the line for his country. As such, his declaration on the mark of the Beast needs to be analyzed with these facts in mind. It should not be passed off as inconsequential chatter and neither should it be held with the same contempt as one would with the salacious opinions proffered by traitors or charlatans at the time.

The Framers were serious, educated men who were not given to folly or recklessness. The Convention was extremely somber in its proceedings as the Delegates all understood the importance of their task. They understood that should they fail in their goal to produce a document that would create a formidable government, the Union would be lost, and they would succumb to their enemies across the Atlantic. Therefore, we can only come to the conclusion that Delegate Read's comments were not uttered in a passing, trivial fashion.

On a motion to strike the words giving Congress the power to "emit bills of credit on the credit of the US," James Madison explained in a footnote that he voted to strike when he "became satisfied that striking out the words would not disable the government from the use of public notes as far as they could be safe and proper, and would only cut off the pretext for a paper currency, and particularly for making the bills a tender for public or private debts."[1]

Madison also recorded in his notes after the debate on paper money that the power to grant Congress the ability to print paper money in the Constitution was voted down and as such the Congress would **NOT** have the power; thereby making gold and silver the only money authorized by the Constitution. Specifically, Madison noted that by deleting the words "and emit bills on the credit of the U.S." from Article I, Section 8, it "would only cut off the pretext for a paper currency and particularly for making the bills a tender either for public or private debts." James Madison's Notes of the Constitutional Convention, August 16, 1787.

---

[1] https://fee.org/articles/the-constitution-and-paper-money/

It is important to point out as well that Madison's notes do not reflect derision for Delegate Read's comments either. Madison merely records it as it was spoken. There is no expanded discussion on the matter in Madison's notes, but obviously there was something to the comment or Delegate Read would not have made it, and Madison would not have recorded it had he believed it to be inconsequential or lunacy. History has, therefore, left us alone in our pursuits to try and discover Delegate Read's meaning.

Being an educated person, Delegate Read was obviously aware of the failed monetary policies of the Continental Congress used during the Revolutionary War, when it began printing paper "Continentals." By 1778, a Continental dollar was worth about 25 cents in gold or silver before its devaluation. It got so bad that by 1781, the Continental Congress itself, you know the guys who printed it to begin with, no longer accepted its own Continentals in payment of debts thereby allowing the Continental's value slip into oblivion.

Delegate Read was also most assuredly aware of its practice and use by other governments throughout the world. Paper banknotes were first issued in Britain shortly after the establishment of the Bank of England in 1694. The use of paper money began to take place in other European countries and spread to the New World by the 1680s. The first instance of paper money in Europe allegedly occurred in Spain in 1438 during a Moorish invasion. A Spanish military leader issued paper notes to his soldiers that circulated around the city.[2]

Yet, none of that history seemed to negate the concerns that Delegate Read had specifically for the newly created United States of America. He was ascribing the prophecy to our new

---

[2] https://www.bullionvault.com/goldnews/paper_money_010720091

nation and none of the others who had also been using paper money. What was so significant about the new nation being formed by the Framers and why was it so important to keep the new nation from having the power to print paper money, while not having the same import with all the other nations that were doing the same thing? Most assuredly, Delegate Read was familiar with the written word in the Bible and clearly recognized what many have failed to see about prophecy and the United States. Frankly, it is absurd to believe that the greatest nation in the history of the world would have been overlooked in the scriptures.

The Framers were well aware of our Nation's destiny and its prophetic rise to power and glory. Hamilton noted in the very first letter of the Federalist Papers that "It has been frequently remarked that it seems to have been reserved to the people of this country, by their conduct and example, to decide the important question, whether societies of men are really capable or not of establishing good government from reflection and choice, or whether they are forever destined to depend for their political constitutions on accident and force." Hamilton, The Federalist Papers, Ltr. 1, 1.

John Jay echoed this sentiment when he wrote that "This country and this people seem to have been made for each other, and it appears as if it was **the design of Providence**, that an inheritance so proper and convenient for a band of brethren, united to each other by the strongest ties, should never be split into a number of unsocial, jealous, and alien sovereignties." Jay, The Federalist Papers, Ltr. 2, 6. (emphasis added)

Finally, Hamilton predicted that we as a nation would "soar to a dangerous greatness." Hamilton, The Federalist Papers, Ltr. 11, 2. Jefferson also implied that we were the new nation of Israel during his Second Inaugural speech: "I shall need, too, the favor of that Being in whose hands we are, who led our fathers, ***as Israel of old***, from their native land and planted them in a country flowing with all the necessaries and comforts of life," (emphasis added) Jefferson, Second Inaugural Address. Delegate Read was obviously filled with these same sentiments.

I should note, however, that prophecy, once spoken, is rarely understood upon its fulfillment. Those who anticipate the fulfillment of prophecy are the ones least likely to recognize it when it finally does occur. Perhaps this statement offends you? I don't know. If so, perhaps we could revisit the prophetic arrival of Christ Himself to the religiously driven Jews who, while waiting for His prophetic arrival, actually rejected Him when He did show up. They did not see His arrival as the fulfillment of prophecy. Perhaps we could also revisit the story of the ancient Israelites who waited four hundred years for their Deliverer, only to reject him as well. They actually fulfilled prophecy by rejecting him and were unable to see it. According to the Book of Acts, when Moses arrived, the Israelites "***understood not***" that he "would deliver them" (Acts 7:25). Yes, it is the way of things. The establishment/status quo always gets it wrong. As Isaiah notes, they that lead thee cause thee to err. (Is. 9:16)

Now, if one takes a serious look at Delegate Read's comment during the debate, it should become quite clear that he was not speculating on the different ways the prophecy could be fulfilled much like many of our leaders do today. Everyone has a theory, right? Delegate Read's tone, however, shows that he was actually speaking prophetically and not theoretically like the neophytes in our day. No, Delegate Read was most definitely not speculating. Obviously, he had some insight into this topic or he wouldn't have raised it in such a vital setting as the Constitutional

Convention. He was a serious, educated Patriot who had sacrificed everything for his country. He was not the kind of person given to sensationalism.

Let me explain. Delegate Read predicted that if the new government of the United States had the power to create paper money it "would be," he argued, as alarming as the mark of the Beast—not "could be," not "might be" or even "can be." He deliberately used the phrase "would be." "Would be" is part of a future tense that indicates that an act will take place in the future. The other phrases—could be, might be, or can be – are used when speaking about possibilities only. Delegate Read emphatically used the phrase "would be." Obviously, he saw something two hundred and thirty-seven years ago that few, if any, can see today now that Congress has been printing paper money for well over one hundred and fifty-two years.

Just like the Jews and the Israelites who sat around waiting for the fulfillment of prophecy without being able to see it when it actually did happen, many in the Christian community are currently waiting around speculating on the fulfillment of this prophecy. Like their predecessors, today's leaders are completely off base being unable to see the literal fulfillment of the mark of the Beast right before their very eyes. Again, like their predecessors, today's leaders have been unable to see our part in the fulfillment of this prophecy. Delegate Read saw it nearly a quarter of a millennium ago, but we have been completely blind to it.

Of course, you are asking yourself, how could the U.S. paper dollar be the mark of the Beast? After all, the U.S. dollar is the king of currencies. We've built our entire economy on the back of the paper dollar, and it has facilitated great economic growth and wealth, right? After all, we have been able to control the world's financial institutions with the paper dollar thereby keeping the world's markets stabilized. Anyone can see that this stabilization resulted from using the paper dollar as the world's reserve currency, correct? No other currency was strong enough and so only the dollar bill could have been used with which to buy and sell internationally. Perhaps it would be good to pause just a bit and reflect.

Let me just say, before we go down that scriptural analysis road, that the Framers were very serious on the issue of paper money. In fact, they were so serious that they outright rejected the proposal to authorize Congress with the power to print paper money. That's not all. They also prohibited the States from exercising the same powers. Madison explained it this way: "The power to make anything but gold and silver a tender in payment of debts, is withdrawn from the States, on the same principle with that of issuing a paper currency." Madison, The Federalist Papers, Ltr. 44, 4. As you can see, this was serious business for the Framers. Unfortunately, no one today even has an inkling with respect to our monetary history.

History has become our Achilles' heel along with our inability to apply it to prophecy. Today's religious influencers will confine their interpretation to only one definition of the word "mark." They believe that the mark spoken of in the Book of Revelation means a symbol, a name or other identifier such as a logo, a visible trace or impression such as a line, a spot or a number, letter or symbol. In light of this common definition, these influencers have glaumed onto physical markers like computer chips or tattoos to explain the meaning of the mark of the Beast.

There is another more relevant definition of the Mark that is rarely, if ever, brought up by the influencers. It is the definition that Delegate Read obviously had in mind, when he made his remark about the paper dollar. The word "Mark" has been referred to as a country's currency since the eleventh century. The mark was used in Germany, Scotland, the birthplace of King James, and it was also used to define the value of the official gold and silver currencies of the Holy Roman Empire. Once this correct definition of the word is understood, the prophecy takes on a whole new meaning in light of Delegate Read's comments. With this definition in mind and the destiny of the new country they were establishing, we can begin to understand why Delegate George Read was so concerned about the Mark of the Beast, when the Convention was debating whether or not Congress should be given the power to print a paper currency. He obviously understood the correct definition of the word and somehow knew that its use here in the United States would fulfill the prophecy.

The enlightened reader should now be asking the question – if the power to print paper money was not put into the Constitution for the Congress and also prohibited the States from doing it, how did our economy become based entirely on the paper dollar, and how does its use fulfill the prophecy of which Delegate Read spoke? The answer will be found with a deeper dive into our history.

Chapter 2
History Is Often Rewritten

"That which hath been is now; and that which is to be hath already been; **and God requireth that which is past.***"*
Ecclesiastes 3:15 (cf. 1:9)

History does repeat itself as "the Preacher" so eloquently taught. Yet, it is equally true that tyrants for generations have repeatedly tried to rewrite history. This book exposes the efforts of corrupt politicians, historians, and bankers who have reshaped our monetary history in order to cover up their crimes. It is my intent to enlarge the memory of the Christian patriot in this regard and to help revive a renewed understanding of how far we have strayed from the righteousness established by our Founders in our founding documents. With this understanding, it is my prayer that patriots will rise up and not rest until our Constitutional Republic is restored in its fulness.

The foundation of our monetary history can be summed up with one short sentence found in the 1844 Supreme Court case *Gwin v. Breedlove,* 43 U.S. (2 How.) 29 (1844) (hereinafter *Gwin*), wherein the U.S. Supreme Court (hereinafter SCOTUS) wrote, "By the Constitution of the United States, gold and silver coins made current by law can only be tendered in payment of debts." In other words, all transactions were done with gold and silver coins and NOT with paper money. Everyone understood that paper currency was not allowed under the U.S. Constitution.

Daniel Webster, who was one of our greatest U.S. Senators, eloquently affirmed this lost truth. He was unrivalled as an orator and a statesman. He was also an attorney who lived and served in the early nineteenth century and eloquently noted on the Senate floor what everyone knew at the time – Congress "clearly has no power to substitute paper, or anything else, for coin, as a tender in payment of debts and discharge of contracts." (Daniel Webster, in a speech before the Senate on December 21, 1836. From A plea for the Constitution of the U.S. of America: wounded in the house of its Guardians by George Bancroft, pp. 93-94.)

He went on to argue that this principle was actually "sacred" and should be held as such at all costs: "The legal tender, therefore, the constitutional standard of value, is established and cannot be overthrown. To overthrow it, would shake the whole system. The constitutional tender is the thing to be preserved, and it ought to be preserved sacredly, under all circumstances." *Id.* (emphasis added) Unfortunately, his counsel along with the Constitution itself were ignored thirty five years later by a rogue Supreme Court which lacked the same respect for our sacred founding document. As a result, our economic system has been shaken many times since that fateful moment. It has ripped us from our Constitutional core and thrown us into a lawless, war-driven economy that has swung wide open the door for our national government to run wild with no limitations on its powers.

Innately sensing the dangers from unchecked spending, our country's citizens constantly look to the corrupt politicians in every election cycle for help. These naïve citizens unwisely believe the lies of the politicians they elect, the ones who promised during their campaigns that they will clean up Washington and stop unchecked spending. Unfortunately, nothing ever happens. Things just get worse.

It was unthinkable just a few years ago that we would see government's runaway spending reach not just millions, nor even billions, but it has crossed over into TRILLIONS and TRILLIONS of dollars. These amounts are unfathomable. Yet, the corrupt politicians appropriate and spend as if our doomsday will never come.

During our annual elections, the politicians run around screaming about the reckless spending in Washington only to participate in the spending sprees once they do get elected. Some actually call for balancing the budget or even an amendment to the Constitution that would require a balanced budget, but no one EVER talks about the real problem – it's not the spending, stupid! The problem is and always has been the paper dollar, but you will never hear anyone admit to it. No one talks about this fact either because no one knows our history or they know it but would never admit it. The reality is that things are only going to get worse until we have a financial collapse from which there will be no return.

Now, I know that you were never taught the real history behind our monetary policies in school. I also know that, right now, you are thinking to yourself that, while it is true that we have our problems, still we are not completely lawless nor are we war-driven. With respect to the lawlessness, I have already dealt extensively with that topic in my prior work *Spectacles of Turbulence and Contention* (hereinafter *Spectacles*), so I am going to focus mainly on our war-driven economy and the coming permanent financial collapse in this work.

Chapter 3
It Will Ever Have

*"Paper money has had the effect in your state **that it will ever have**, to ruin commerce, oppress the honest, and open the door to every species of fraud and injustice."*
George Washington,
Letter to Jabez Bowen,
9 January 1787

Paper money is and always has been unconstitutional. As discussed in the previous chapters, the Framers made sure that Congress would have absolutely no power to authorize the use of paper money, or anything else, as a legal tender in payment of debts and discharge of contracts except for gold and silver coins. This historical fact was affirmed not only by members of Congress, such as Daniel Webster, but also by SCOTUS in the 1844 *Gwin* case. Only gold and silver coin can constitutionally be used as a legal tender despite what we are doing now. The States were also prohibited by the Constitution from using anything other than silver and gold as well.

If using unauthorized tender were the only part of the Constitution being completely ignored by the federal government, which it is not, that one unauthorized act would still be important enough to qualify as complete lawlessness.

Unfortunately, it is not the only part of the Constitution that has been discarded by the corrupt DC establishment.

As you will find in *Spectacles*, not only has every major provision of the U.S. Constitution been changed through practice rather than by amendment as required by the Constitution, but many of the minor provisions have been unlawfully changed as well. We truly have arrived at a point where the Constitution is adhered to in name only. I don't care what the dishonest politicians may say otherwise. Remember this one thing, if nothing else, politicians profess reverence to the Constitution as long as it remains shut.

With respect to the topic at hand, it is vital to always remember that the Framers despised paper currency despite what the revisionists may say about it today. James Madison wrote that any attempts by the government to authorize the use of "paper money" is a "wicked project." Madison, The Federalist Papers, Ltr. 10, 22. James Madison is referred to as the Father of Constitution, since he was the chief architect behind it, so his words alone should carry the day on this topic, but he wasn't the only one who felt this way. Madison even went so far as to call it a pestilence--"the prohibition to bills of credit must give pleasure to every citizen" due to the fact that America had sustained such a great loss "from the pestilent effects of paper money" during the Revolutionary War. Madison, The Federalist Papers, Ltr. 44, 4. (emphasis added) He continued his attack on paper currency by declaring that it would destroy the "morals of the people, and on the character of republican government." Id.

Our Constitutional Republican government's true character has been erased and substituted with a very flawed, weak, and dangerous hybrid form of democracy. Unfortunately, few if any understand this important fact. The morals of the people, just as

Madison warned, have also been ruined with the transition to paper money. We have become a society obsessed with materialism and hedonistic pleasures driven entirely by an insatiable thirst for money.

It wasn't just Madison who felt this way about the paper dollar. The overwhelming majority of the Founders hated paper currency as well, including our great first president whose portrait was involuntarily appropriated and emblazoned on every dollar bill for the whole world to see. Yes, it is true. The image of the man whom King George once referred to as "the Greatest Man in the world" has been inexorably tied to the pestilence and wickedness of the paper dollar by having his face etched forever on the front side of the dollar bill. If the truth were known and adhered to, it would never have happened.

In a letter to Jabez Bowen dated January 9, 1787, George Washington wrote that "Paper money has had the effect in your State that it ever will have, to ruin commerce—oppress the honest, and open a door to every species of fraud and injustice." This does not sound like it was written by a man who wanted his face on the paper dollar. There is no wiggle room at all to argue otherwise. Given his strong position on the matter, it is impossible to imagine that our greatest President's face would have ever ended up on the paper dollar with his consent. No doubt, the whole thing was concocted as a way to create the illusion of legitimacy. In monetary circles, this would be known as a counterfeit narrative!

Thomas Jefferson felt basically the same way. "Paper is poverty," he argued in 1788. "It is only the ghost of money, and not money itself." Later in 1817, he wrote that "Paper money's abuses also are inevitable and, by breaking up the measure of value, make a lottery of all private property."[3]

Now I know the arguments made by our Founders against paper currency fly in the face of today's monetary theory "experts," so, history had to be rewritten. The money changers needed a different story in order to perpetrate their immoral, unconstitutional fraud on the world. By placing Washington's face on the dollar, the past was unalterably changed... forever. With his face on the front of the dollar bill, it sent their duplicitous message to the world that Washington approved of paper currency. It also added legitimacy. No one could question the validity of their unconstitutional actions with his face firmly on the front of the paper dollar bill – no one.

The fraudsters needed to send a strong message to anyone who dared to question their funny money. After all, if the face of our country's greatest President was on the dollar bill, it clearly meant that Washington approved of the measure. Just look! Anyone saying otherwise would be labeled unpatriotic or as someone who would defame our first great President. They conflated the paper dollar into the man himself, never to be separated again. These fraudsters made sure that the real history was never taught again – anywhere.

In fact, there are prominent conservatives among us today – you know, conservatives who say they believe in the original intent of our Founding Fathers – who will tell you that "the paper dollar is our greatest export." Yet, this kind of thinking flies in the face of what Washington and the Founders actually believed and taught.

---

[3] https://www.nationalreview.com/2011/07/founders-no-fans-paper-currency-deroy-murdock/

If we were to take a minute to look back over the last one hundred and ten years or so, it would be impossible to argue that Washington and the other Founders were wrong about paper money, unless, of course, you skipped your history class in high school and therein lies the irony. By rewriting our history about the truth of paper money, the real history since its implementation bears witness that paper money leaves a path of death, destruction, and economic catastrophes in its wake thereby validating the warnings of our founders. Yet, no one knows the connection since we have lost our sense of history.

We've had an unending string of wars since its inception. Our nation's economy has been wiped out time and time again over the last one hundred years, and all because of paper money. Remember the stock market crash of 1929? What about the Great Depression of 1932-1936? What about the runaway inflation of the 1970s? What about the stock market crash of 1989? How about the colossal crash of 2008? What about the steady devaluation of the dollar along with the rise of inflation? Oh, and then there is the fraud and injustice of which Washington spoke. The politicians authorize trillions of dollars, and the trillions of dollars are paid out only to be laundered back into their own pockets and the pockets of their donors. Can anyone say Ukraine?

All the while, the People's financial lives have been ruined by these shell games, historic crashes, and inflationary periods. The honest citizens who have scrimped and saved their whole lives have seen the value of their money dissipate like vapor, while the fraudsters running our financial institutions have made off like robber barons just as Washington predicted.

Under the U.S. Mint Act of 1792, the dollar was pegged at 24.75 grains of Gold. There are 480 grains in a troy ounce. Thus it took $19.40 to purchase a single troy ounce of gold with one dollar. As of January 2009, it took $864 to purchase that same troy ounce of gold, which represents a 97.8% drop in value.[4] That's a heck of a loss in value. It's pretty close to 100%.

Another disturbing statistic shows that 1% of the population in the U.S. owns most of the wealth in this country. The bottom 50% of the population owns only 1.5% of the wealth. These few statistics alone prove Washington's point that paper money oppresses the honest because of fraud and injustice. Of course, the socialists and the commies want to blame the free market system for the disparities, but the problem is the paper dollar and those who get to control it.

It has been reported that John Maynard Keynes, the man who started it all said: "Lenin was certainly right, there is no more positive, or subtle means of destroying the existing basis of society than to debauch the currency. By a continuing process of inflation, governments can confiscate secretly and unobserved an important part of the wealth of the citizens. The process engages all the hidden forces of economics on the side of destruction, and does it in a manner that not one man in a million can diagnose." (Economic consequences of the Peace) (attributed to Bill Murphy of GATA, for this quote, at www.lemetropolecafe.com) Whether he actually said it or not is irrelevant as the statement is still true.

Speaking of today, inflation has been running amok and ruining commerce once again. Gas prices are at levels never before seen. We are at forty-year highs with inflation. The price of eggs alone is at unheard of prices. Milton Friedman once famously said that "Inflation is always and everywhere a monetary phenomenon." In other words, it is a paper money problem. You keep printing money. You keep getting inflation.

---

[4] https://www.bullionvault.com/goldnews/paper_money_010720091

Yes, yes, I know that there are plenty of economic "experts" out there who believe otherwise. These experts will give you their discombobulated reasons as to why Friedman was wrong. When listening to their lengthy and complex explanations, however, you most likely find yourself confused. The best explanation of any phenomenon is the one that makes the fewest assumptions. Also known as Occam's razor, it means that the simplest answer is most likely the correct one. Friedman and Washington's simple answers were the right ones – it's the paper money. It always has been and always will be the problem.

Even now, many financial "experts" are predicting a total collapse of our financial system. Reasons for this so-called coming collapse are varied. Many believe that it is being orchestrated by some dark globalist cabal, but if you knew your monetary history, you'd know that Washington was right, and that it is not some dark, globalist conspiracy. Our commerce has been and will continue to be destroyed by the paper dollar and the fraud upon which it is permanently fixed.

Chapter 4
Acts of Usurpation

*"These will be merely acts of usurpation, and **will be deserved to be treated as such**."*
Hamilton, Federalist No. 33 7

Nearly twenty years after the decision in the *Gwin* case, the corrupt politicians in Washington, DC ran into a huge problem. They had a war on their hands and funds were tight – what they really wanted was a blank check to pay for it all. The Constitution and *Gwin's* reaffirmation of the Constitutional rule against paper money was the only thing standing in the way of their thirst and love for an unlimited supply of money. Thankfully, for them, as any serious politician understands, they knew how to manipulate any good crisis to their benefit. It was Rahm Emanuel who famously exposed the corrupt politicians' creed and the reason for it – corrupt politicians, he explained, will always use a good crisis to do things that they couldn't possibly do otherwise.

Politicians love paper money more than anything else. They love it because it lets them spend, spend, spend, and then spend some more. Spending is to politicians what water is to fish. They can't survive without it. Remember how Paul told us that the love of money is the root of all evil? Well, the corrupt politicians at the time of the Civil War knew that they couldn't legally print paper money, but they knew that the crisis of the Civil War had provided them with a glorious opportunity to make it happen.

It should come as no surprise, then, to learn how quickly a politician came up with a Legislative Bill at the beginning of the Civil War to simply ignore the Constitution and just start the printing presses before anybody could stop them. The rules were no longer necessary and neither were gold nor silver – they had a genuine crisis on their hands! The politicians argued at the time that it was a one-of-a-kind emergency and so they could print paper money for as long as the crisis lasted.

Seriously, have you ever heard of a politician who relinquished power once it had been acquired? Yeah, neither have I. Anyway, our politician's name was Elbridge Gerry Spaulding and, I know that this will come as a shock to you, but Spaulding also just happened to be a banker. What an amazing coincidence that it was a banker who came up with the idea to print tons of paper money. There was obviously no conflict of interest there, right? Anyway, as the Chairman of the House Ways and Means Subcommittee on Banking and Currency, Spaulding introduced a bill to start printing paper money, because, as he put, it was a "measure of necessity" for the "war."

Spaulding was no dummy. He knew full well that his position was radical. He knew that it was a proposition that went against all things Constitutional, but he didn't let that dissuade him. "These are extraordinary times," he argued, "and extraordinary measures must be resorted to, in order to save our government." What a guy, huh? I mean, he only wanted to save the country, and I'm sure, as a banker, his heroic measures would not have benefited him in the least.

The purpose of the bill simply authorized the department of the Treasury to issue $150,000,000 in paper notes as "lawful money and a legal tender in payment of all debts, public and private, within the United States." Just like that there was $150 million magically poofed into existence, thus, avoiding the dreaded tax increase on the frontend that would have been necessary, had they kept to the Constitution. Spaulding knew that inflation would take care of the tax increase on the public later down the road with no one the wiser.

The United States federal notes that Congress authorized, which were informally known as "greenbacks," since they were printed with green ink, were not backed by specie—i.e., gold or silver coin. In other words, the greenbacks were nothing more than green-colored funny money.

Once the bill was passed, Spaulding only had one problem left and that was to convince Lincoln's Secretary of the Treasury to go along with the scheme. His name was Salmon P. Chase and, since Chase was a bit of an originalist, Spaulding knew it was going to be a tough sell. History shows that Secretary Chase was extremely reluctant to the idea, but he was eventually swayed by Spaulding's arguments and, therefore, acknowledged that the situation had become "indispensably necessary that we should resort to the issue of United States notes." The Bill was passed by Congress and signed into law by President Lincoln on February 25, 1862, otherwise was known as the Legal Tender Act.[5]

With the paper money matter settled and out of the way, the country was able to get into the business of making some serious war, that is, as long as they could keep their paper money machine alive and didn't let some do-good attorney try to stop them with a lawsuit. One such lawsuit was actually filed in 1862

---

[5]https://archive.nytimes.com/opinionator.blogs.nytimes.com/2013/12/31/the-birth-of-the-greenback/

in New York, which challenged the constitutionality of Spaulding's Act.

It was the New York Supreme Court and not SCOTUS, however, that ruled that the funny money Act was constitutional, but this is where the story gets even more crazy. The case was actually appealed to SCOTUS because, well, it violated the Constitution on its face, like everyone knew it did, and SCOTUS was the supreme court of the land. SCOTUS also knew it was unconstitutional and that was a huge problem, so they had to come up with a plan to avoid hearing the appeal.

This is the point where everything was thrown out the window. The money interests argued incredulously that SCOTUS actually "lacked jurisdiction to hear the appeal because it could not review a decision by the highest court of any state that upheld a federal statute." *Id.* Yeah, that's the worst legal argument I've ever heard, since SCOTUS is the highest court in the land and not the NY Supreme Court, but SCOUTUS loved it, and just like that, the Legal Tenders Act was never challenged in front of SCOTUS.

On December 18, 1863, SCOTUS agreed with the insane argument that SCOTUS lacked the jurisdiction to hear a case where the New York Supreme Court, an inferior court, basically overturned the SCOTUS' decision in *Gwin*. With that decision, SCOTUS basically said that whenever a lower court overturns a U.S. Supreme Court decision, the U.S. Supreme Court can't do anything about it. Do you see the sleight of hand here? They had to have their paper money scam no matter what and, obviously, the courts were in on the fraud and had no problem accommodating the paper money cartel.

One of the Justices on the Court at the time, apparently trying to justify SCOTUS's betrayal of the Constitution, would later argue that their "judicial dodge," as he called it, was a "fortuitous reprieve" because "the rebellion would have triumphed… the national government would have perished, and, with it, the Constitution." *Id.*

Of course, this argument is nothing more than poppycock, since it is impossible to actually know if the South's rebellion would have triumphed if the North had not started printing paper money. It is pure speculation. One thing is certain, since that decision, we have seen the national government become all-powerful, and the Constitution itself has become nothing more than a piece of parchment to which politicians pay lip service. In saving the national government with their "judicial dodge," they actually destroyed our Constitution and the Republic along with it, because this "judicial dodge" was not a one-time event. SCOTUS has used it many other times.

Most recently, SCOTUS used it during the 2020 election, when Texas AG Paxton filed a lawsuit against several other states for violating the Constitutional rights of their citizens. Even though the Constitution expressly states that SCOTUS has original jurisdiction in cases where a State is the party, they used the "judicial dodge" in Paxton's case, much like it did in 1862, arguing that Texas lacked standing to bring the case. I mean, hey the fraudsters had to get rid of Trump somehow, right? They just needed another "judicial dodge" to do it and voila! No more Trump.

I wonder if one of the Justices on the Supreme Court will ever try and make the same argument as they did about the 1862 dodge. I can just hear it now. Justice Roberts arguing in his memoirs that their "judicial dodge" in 2020 was necessary to keep the fascist Trump out of Washington thereby saving the national government once again.

Are you beginning to see the problem here?

Chapter 5
Many Who Doubted Yielded Their Doubts

"It is not surprising that amid the tumult of the late civil war, and under the influence of apprehensions for the safety of the Republic almost universal, different views, never before entertained by American statesmen or jurists, were adopted by many... Many who doubted yielded their doubts; many who did not doubt were silent. Some who were strongly averse to making government notes a legal tender felt themselves constrained to acquiesce in the views of the advocates of the measure."
Hepburn v. Griswold,
75 U.S. (8 Wall.) 603 67 (1870)

Once the Civil War ended, the bankers and the politicians knew that they were not out of the woods yet with respect to their fraudulent money deal. The decision to allow paper money had only been justified by the emergencies created by the Civil War. Since the war was over, the paper money cartel knew that justification for their constitutional subversion was at an end but the politicians didn't want to let go of their funny money. They wanted to keep on spending without the restrictions of the Constitution, so they had to come up with a new argument in order to justify keeping their paper money forever.

Why would they, you might ask? Well, throughout history, paper money has always been used for one major purpose—it has always been used to wage war wherein the bankers are prone to fund both sides of a conflict and make off like bandits. Now, in case you missed it, politicians are masters at getting what they want even when there is nearly one hundred years of well-established constitutional law standing in their way. Of course, there were legal challenges that arose in an effort to check their destructive measures, but the corrupt politicians would not let that deter them from getting what they wanted.

No doubt, there were some Constitutionalists who had caved to the arguments in favor of paper money caused by the pressures of the Civil War. These individuals knew that the Constitution did not give the national government the power to print paper money, but they caved to the paper money cartel and their arguments out of fear.

Fear is a great tool for politicians, and they are very adept at using it. When decisions are based on fear, they are always wrong. Secretary Chase was one of those individuals who caved into the fear. He gave his consent to the paper money hysteria, even though he knew it was wrong and not authorized by the Constitution. He had bought into the argument that the North would lose the war if they didn't use paper money to fuel the war effort.

Following the war, however, there was a very interesting turn of events. Lincoln appointed Treasury Secretary Chase to be the Chief Justice of the United States Supreme Court in 1864. It was during his tenure as Chief Justice that he had the chance to correct the fatal monetary decision he made as Secretary of the Treasury. You will recall that he reluctantly gave his consent to Spaulding's Legal Tender Bill in 1862, but, as the Chief Justice of the U.S. Supreme Court, he remedied that decision in 1869 with the Court's ruling in *Hepburn v. Griswold*, 75 U.S. 603 (1869) (hereinafter *Griswold*). *Griswold* held that a citizen of the United States was no longer legally obligated to accept the government's paper money. As such, Spaulding's Legal Tender Act was not the law of the land under that ruling.

The Chief Justice was no longer acting as a politician as he did when he was Secretary of the Treasury. Under *Griswold*, the Chief Justice reverted back to being a legal scholar. He could no longer tolerate the legal fiction that had enveloped the country from the chaos of the Civil War and the unconstitutional policies that rose out of that war. Like pretty much everyone else, Secretary Chase admitted that he had been pressured by the paper money cartel and reluctantly gave his consent. Even at that time, he knew that Spaulding's funny money law was patently unconstitutional, but he had always been for the Constitution as he explained in *Griswold*:

"It is not surprising that amid the tumult of the late civil war, and under the influence of apprehensions for the safety of the Republic almost universal, different views, never before entertained by American statesmen or jurists, were adopted by many... Many who doubted yielded their doubts; many who did not doubt were silent. Some who were strongly averse to making government notes a legal tender felt themselves constrained to acquiesce in the views of the advocates of the measure." *Griswold*, at 67.

Griswold had finally corrected the matter and firmly settled any questions as to where Chief Justice Chase's loyalties lay:

"Not a few who then insisted upon its necessity, or acquiesced in that view, have, since the return of peace, and under the influence of the calmer time, reconsidered their

conclusions, and now concur in those which we have just announced. These conclusions seem to us to be fully sanctioned by the letter and spirit of the Constitution." Id.

This decision was definitely a blow to the paper money interests, but it wouldn't last long.

Chapter 6
In Any Emergency

> *"If it be held by this court that Congress has no constitutional power,* under any circumstances, or *in any emergency, to make treasury notes a legal tender for the payment of all debts (a power confessedly possessed by every independent sovereignty other than the United States), the government is without those means of self-preservation."*
> Knox v. Lee,
> 79 U.S. 457,529 (1871)

As discussed previously, the creed of every politician is to never let a good crisis go to waste. Whenever a crisis is declared (real or otherwise), politicians, like chicken little, will run around screaming that all will be lost if they are not given emergency powers in order to become saviors for the people in handling the crisis which invariably confronts them.

This fact was never more apparent than during the late Covid-19 crisis of 2020 and beyond. Every politician from mayors, to governors, to the President, and to the Deep State bureaucrats jumped on the chicken little bandwagon to exercise their unconstitutional "emergency" powers in order to shut down small businesses, churches, schools, and individual lives. The few voices who tried to warn the public about the dangers of complying with those unconstitutional acts were ignored, discredited, or even silenced. Except for those few voices, basically, the entire U.S. population unwittingly and passively went along with everything they were told to do by their overlords. There was no violent uprising. There was no effective organized resistance to any of the mandates. There was very little pounding of the pulpits from our religious leaders like those prior to 1776. There was basically nothing but silent compliance from religious and community leaders to the general populace. Yes, you should all be embarrassed, but I digress.

James Madison warned us that our liberties would be lost with the use of these kinds of tactics. When making an appeal to the Virginia Constitutional Convention for support in ratifying the newly proposed U.S. Constitution on June 6, 1788, Madison actually expressed his doubts as to the longevity of the Republic with the somber warning that "There are more instances of the abridgment of the freedom of the people *by gradual and silent encroachments of those in power*, than by violent and sudden usurpations." (emphasis added)

A review of the last one hundred and fifty years easily reveals to the willing eye all of those *gradual and silent encroachments* that have been employed by the politicians. Such a review makes it easy to see why we so willingly and so easily gave up our freedoms during the Covid-19 emergency and the obvious stolen elections that took place during that time. No doubt, we will most likely fall prey again, when the next emergency rolls around.

This willing and silent compliance by the masses and our leaders all started with the Civil War crisis wherein the American people chose to go along with the politicians and their justifications for ignoring the Constitution in order to give

Congress emergency powers to print paper money. There was no uprising in spite of the fact that everyone knew that paper money was not allowed under the Constitution. No one took to the streets. No one. It was just willing and silent compliance much like we've seen with every other silent encroachment on the Constitution.

Looking back, it would appear that the last time the federal government actually recognized the constitutional limitation of its powers was in 1919 during the ratification of the 18th Amendment. The period of time covered by the 18th Amendment has come to be known as the period of "Prohibition." This Amendment to the U.S. Constitution was ratified by the necessary number of states on January 19, 1919. It has been referred to as "Prohibition" simply because it prohibited the manufacture, sale, and transportation of alcoholic beverages within the United States.

In December of 1933, Prohibition ended when Utah gave the 36th and final vote for ratification of the 21st Amendment. The history buffs will tell you that the 18th Amendment was driven mainly by the temperance movements of the day. They will tell you that it became a battle between the "wet" and the "dry" states – the "dry" states wanted to enforce their ideas of temperance and morality on everyone else, while the wet states pushed back arguing for individual freedom and choice. Yes, these narratives are a description of the forces operating back then, but they are not the reason we have the 18th Amendment.

As James Madison explained to the members of the Virginia Constitutional Convention on June 6, 1788 "the powers of the Federal government are enumerated; it can only operate in certain cases: it has legislative powers on defined and limited objects, ***beyond which it cannot extend its jurisdiction.***" (emphasis added)

In other words, if the power is not specifically defined and listed in the Constitution, Congress cannot legally extend its reach. In fact, Madison explained that the powers granted to the Congress were "few and defined" – "The powers delegated by the proposed Constitution to the Federal Government, are *few and defined*. Those which are to remain in the State Governments are numerous and indefinite." Madison, The Federalist Papers, Ltr. 45, 9. (emphasis added)

Madison went further and spelled out exactly what those "few and defined" powers were so as to leave no room for speculation. The Federal government's powers, he wrote, "Will be exercised principally on external objects, as war, peace, negotiation, and foreign commerce." *Id.*

Have you ever even heard of such a thing in today's political environment? Seriously, do you ever hear anyone raise the issue of constitutional authority before Congress passes any law nowadays? Today, everything is regulated by Congress. It is no longer "on external objects," but they have taken over the States' position which are numerous and indefinite.

For example, with regards to the 18th Amendment, if you will just take a little time to read it, you will find that there is not a single word in the Constitution that pertains to the manufacture, sale, and transportation of alcohol outside of the 18th Amendment, and this is the real reason we have the 18th Amendment. Under the Constitution, Congress clearly and undeniably lacks the authority or power to pass any law prohibiting the manufacture, sale, and transportation of alcohol except as given by the 18th Amendment. Everyone understood this fact and that is why we have the 18th Amendment. One only has to look to the language found in the 18th Amendment to understand. Specifically, the 18th Amendment gives legislative power to the Congress in Section 2 of that Amendment: "The Congress and the several States shall have concurrent power to enforce this article by appropriate legislation."

This language clearly shows that Congress did not have the authority to pass legislation regulating alcohol before passage of the 18th Amendment. Tragically, the passage of the 18th Amendment was the last time Congress ever really felt the need to attain specific authorization under the Constitution to pass any law. I guess the mood in Congress became one of convenience.

What is even more mind-blowing is how few people in the United States even care about or even understand how far Congress has exceeded its authority. Now, couple that with the implausible fact that Congress passed the exact same law as the 18th Amendment in 1970 without feeling any need whatsoever to consult with the States or the American people through the Amendment process in order to acquire the necessary authority for the 1970 law. One can only wonder in amazement as to what changed between 1917 and 1970.

Otherwise known as the Controlled Substances Act (CSA), this law was passed by Congress in 1970 and prohibits "the manufacture, importation, possession, use, and distribution" of basically every drug known to man on various schedules identified by the Congress. This is almost the exact same language as the 18th Amendment with one exception. The 1970 law authorizes Congress to regulate the manufacture, sale, and distribution of EVERY drug known to man, when it took a full-blown Constitutional amendment just to regulate one drug otherwise known as alcohol.

It's almost as if they started telling themselves behind closed doors that "We'll be damned if we're going to go through that amendment process again!" They knew that they needed a better plan to get around that pesky little list of their "few and defined" powers spelled out in the Constitution. They succeeded, and frankly, it is shocking how far Congress has strayed from the Constitution since that time. Even so-called conservatives don't care about having the power to pass a particular law any more. If it's an important societal issue then the Constitution be damned, and we'll just pass a new law to regulate it because it's important.

MTG is one such example. Held up by many as a conservative firebrand, she has been pushing to pass a law to protect children against the transgender maniacs even though she has been told by some that there is no power to pass it, but she doesn't care. She says it's important. President Trump has also come out and promised to sign that law. There isn't any real daylight between a conservative and liberal any more, but this is where we find ourselves, and it all started with the passage of the Legal Tender Act of 1862.

Even though Chief Justice Chase was able to reverse the unconstitutional actions taken during the Civil War in ***Griswold***, it took just two short years for a larger SCOTUS to take up the exact issue once again. Clearly, the paper money forces were not to be denied their due. The case was known as ***Knox v. Lee***, 79 U.S. 457, 529 (1871) (hereinafter referred to as ***Knox***).

No doubt, there were some dark forces at work for SCOTUS to take up the exact same issue just two years after the prior case had already been decided and especially given the fact that the whole issue had been decided on well settled constitutional law for nearly one hundred years.

In spite of all that history, the **Knox** Court went on to overrule "what was decided in **Hepburn v. Griswold**," *Id.* at 554. They never even discussed the **Gwin** case and simply ignored the legal history that I have presented to you here with respect to paper money. The Justices abandoned their constitutional duty to exercise judgment from the bench so that they could become more of a policymaking body.

In order to reach their policy decision in **Knox**, as you might have already guessed, they had to use another crisis as justification to reauthorize the unconstitutional Legal Tender Act. The **Knox** court explained that if "legal tender notes are rendered unavailable" then "ruinous sacrifices, general distress, and bankruptcy ***may be expected***." *Id.* at 531. See how that works? It wasn't even a fact. It was only a possibility that a crisis "may be expected" that justified their decision.

Once a politician has assumed any kind of power, it is impossible to take it back. It was this moment, I believe, that became the inflection point where the courts and the politicians began to move past our Framers and the Constitution in order to restructure the country in their image. In order to accomplish this restructuring, since the decision in **Knox**, the dark forces have always created a crisis in order to justify their abandonment of the Constitution.

If someone actually does try and take away any newly acquired power as Chief Justice Chase did in **Griswold**, then all that has to be done is to declare another emergency. By the way, it should also be emphasized that there is not a syllable in the Constitution, as Hamilton would say, that mentions emergency powers. There is no such power, and yet it has been used and is still being used to completely destroy the Constitution.

This is what they did in ***Knox***. The ***Knox*** court had no legal justification for their decision, and they knew it, so they declared that there was a crisis in the making. The Court warned that a financial crisis just might actually happen if things went back to the way they were before the Civil War. Horror of horrors! What could be worse than potential "ruinous sacrifices" and "bankruptcy"? Oh and "general distress"? See how that works? Problem solved. How did the country ever survive for one hundred years without paper money?

It is amazing that once paper money had been used, and that, for only eight short years, the court told us that it would be impossible for the country to survive without it, because, well, "ruinous sacrifices" and other horrible things "may be expected"! The truth was, however, that its use had only been justified in 1862 to fight a Civil War as an emergency stop gap only. Once the ***Griswold*** court stopped its use in 1869, the country found out that it couldn't live without it. After all, if the country were forced to stop its use, after only a few short years, then there just might be some "ruinous sacrifices" ahead! The "ruinous sacrifices" that they were most worried about, I'm sure, had to do with the investments made by the bankers and the politicians into the new currency.

There was no historical or legal basis for the court's decision in ***Knox***, but SCOTUS ignored all that and declared that the power to print paper money was a necessary means for the government to preserve itself. This reasoning, of course, is madness, and it opened the door to complete and utter lawlessness. The practical effect of ***Knox's*** ruling was that SCOTUS could now amend the Constitution anytime it likes.

This was exactly the problem Hamilton was talking about in Letter 78 of The Federalist Papers: "The courts must declare the sense of the law; and if they should be disposed to exercise WILL instead of JUDGMENT, the consequence would equally be the substitution of their pleasure to that of the legislative body." Hamilton, The Federalist Papers, Ltr. 78, 16.

The Court was no longer exercising "JUDGMENT." The Court simply and unconstitutionally imposed its "WILL." They wanted a particular outcome so they contrived an obtuse argument to impose their will in the matter.

This danger had actually been talked about prior to the ratification of the Constitution. One of the biggest criticisms of the proposed Constitution was that SCOTUS would become superior to the Congress with their ability to interpret the Constitution according to the spirit of the document and that there would be no recourse to such actions, since the Courts are not elected—they are appointed for life.

Hamilton framed the argument this way: "The authority of the proposed Supreme Court of the United States, which is to be a separate and independent body, will be superior to that of the legislature. The power of construing the laws according to the SPIRIT of the Constitution, will enable that court to mold them into whatever shape it may think proper; especially as its decisions will not be in any manner subject to the revision or correction of the legislative body." Hamilton, The Federalist Papers, Ltr. 81, 3. This argument's rationale is exactly what happened in ***Knox***.

Hamilton was very explicit in his rebuttal to that argument. It was not only without precedent in the history of the judiciary, he exclaimed, but it would also be extremely dangerous and would most definitely not be allowed under the proposed Constitution – "This is as unprecedented as it is dangerous," Hamilton argued, but "upon examination, will be found to be made up altogether of false reasoning upon misconceived fact." *Id.*

As to the spirit of the laws, Hamilton makes this unmistakable clarification to the detractors of his day: "In the first place, there is not a SYLLABLE in the plan under consideration which DIRECTLY empowers the national courts to construe the laws according to the spirit of the Constitution, or which gives them any greater latitude in this respect than may be claimed by the courts of every State." *Id.* at 4. (emphasis added) Yet, since the opinion in **Knox**, SCOTUS has been doing just what Hamilton argued would be impossible to do. The courts have been making policy in order to impose their will "in the spirit of the Constitution," and there has been no recourse to stop them.

In Hamilton's defense, however, he did warn of the perils that would arise if "men disposed to usurp" were appointed to the Bench. Hamilton, The Federalist Papers, Ltr. 84, 2. "Those men disposed to usurp," he explained, "would use anything as 'a plausible pretence for claiming... power' that did not exist, but 'afforded a clear implication, that a power to prescribe proper regulations concerning it was intended to be vested in the national government.'" *Id.*

This is exactly what happened in **Knox** and every other unconstitutional decision by the courts since that time. It was the beginning of the end for the Constitution as usurpers have filled up the benches of our courts for years. With their decision in **Knox**, SCOTUS started their long-term practice of amending the Constitution by Opinion—by imposing their will--which is what they want the Constitution to say rather than adhering to the plain language of the document.

It is insane to believe that the Congress is unable to pass laws that are unconstitutional, which, as you know, SCOTUS will strike down from time-to-time, while at the same believing that everything that SCOTUS does is constitutional, and no one can strike down their decisions even when they are wrong. Yet, that is the state of affairs in which we find ourselves. Whenever SCOTUS acts outside the Constitution as they did in ***Knox***, and in so many other decisions since that time, we just accept those decisions as akin to holy writ and never to be questioned.

The Framers recognized that SCOTUS could act outside of the Constitution just as easily as the Congress. When it happens, Hamilton urged that such acts should be ignored and treated as acts of usurpation: "…it will not follow… that acts… which are NOT PURSUANT to its constitutional powers… will become the supreme law of the land. These will be merely acts of usurpation, and will be deserved to be treated as such." Hamilton, The Federalist Papers, Ltr. 33, 7.

Sadly, no one ever challenges SCOTUS. No one ever ignores their usurpations as Hamilton suggested. It's as if we've all come under some kind of a spell when it comes to SCOTUS. A prime example of this fact was seen in the *Roe v. Wade* decision. We endured that blatantly unconstitutional decision for fifty years and allowed over 60 million babies to be slaughtered in their mothers' wombs. We should never have given that decision any credence whatsoever as it was so blatantly unconstitutional, and it all started with the ***Knox*** decision. Since that time, we've seen the country decay and rot from within to the point where we are approaching our end.

Chapter 7
Gone Down to Hell with Their Weapons of War

*"And they shall not lie with the mighty that are fallen of the uncircumcised, **which are gone down to hell with their weapons of war.**"*
Ezekiel 32:5

As noted, paper money has been around for centuries. It is most definitely NOT a modern innovation. It is nothing new and has always been characterized by economic turbulence, and it has always been used to wage war. For these and other reasons, the Framers excluded the power to use paper money from the Constitution.

Reverting to its use is actually the *outdated* thing to do despite what the economic experts try to tell you. All of our problems today have resulted from ignoring the Constitution and allowing our politicians to act outside of its limitations. By giving the politicians unlimited access to money under **Knox**, SCOTUS forced us back to the old world and its despotic, disastrous practices. Our decay and corruption were actually expected by the Founders. Men like Franklin warned that the people will eventually become so corrupted that they will get what they deserve—despotism:

"In these sentiments, sir, I agree to this Constitution, with all its faults—if they are such; because I think a general Government necessary for us, and there is no form of government but what may be a blessing to the people, **_IF_** well administered; and I believe, farther, that it is likely to be well administered for a course of years, and **_can only end in despotism_**, as other forms have done before it, **_when the people shall become so corrupted as to need despotic government_**, being incapable of any other." (emphasis added) Benjamin Franklin, Speech in the Constitutional Convention, at the Conclusion of its Deliberations, Delivered September 17, 1787.

To anyone with eyes to see, we have arrived at Franklin's *end*. Everything our government has been doing over the last one hundred fifty years has been a move to consolidate power in Washington, DC in order to wage their illegal wars. The Congress has abdicated many of its Constitutional duties and responsibilities under Article I, Sec. 8, while spending all of its time passing laws for which it has no authority, not to mention the time spent on insider trading in order to enrich themselves along with the laundering of money that Congress deceptively labels as "foreign aid."

The President has moved closer and closer to becoming a total monarchy. One of the characteristics of a King, Hamilton noted, was the King's ability to manipulate the economy. According to Hamilton, the King is "the arbiter of commerce." The Federalist Papers, Hamilton, Ltr. 69, 15.

My, oh my, how things have digressed. In today's economy, the President is not only seen as the "arbiter of commerce," but he is completely responsible for it according to the polls. If the economy is bad, it's the President's fault, and he is punished at the polls. If it's great, he takes credit for it and is rewarded at the polls. He appoints the Chairman to the Federal Reserve. The Chairman, at the behest of the President, manipulates the commerce through the money supply and its interest rates. How is this any different than what a King could do according to Hamilton? I know, I know, things are just very different today; that was then, this is now. We're sophisticated and modern, the Founders were backwards and outdated.

Being modern and sophisticated doesn't change the fact that the nation's top executive controls commerce, and Congress prints unlimited, and heretofore, unfathomable, amounts of money while trying to obscure their actions by using terms like "quantitative easing" and "inflation." It's a tax – pure and simple.

The President is our King. He sends his armies and navies around the globe to engage in combat, destroy infrastructure, and destroy lives without Congressional interference or authorization. You should realize that this behavior is the very thing that Jefferson attacked the King of England for doing in the Declaration of Independence.

In short, the U.S. President has been making war for a very, very long time with his unlimited supply of paper money. In fact, the last time Congress actually followed the Constitution and declared war was on December 8, 1941. Since that time, we've decided that the Constitution is, once again, an inconvenience. The President has been waging his unconstitutional wars in Korea, Vietnam, South America, the Middle East, Afghanistan, and now Ukraine – ALL without a formal declaration of war.

Money is no problem, though, so just fire up the proverbial printing presses and give the President what he wants whenever he wants it. With all of that money and war, the President and his military industrial complex have been able to create weapons of war that can kill unlike anything the world has ever known.

If we had been using the money of the Constitution – gold and silver – the Congress would have been forced to overtly raise taxes on the American citizen in order to wage their wars. With paper money, the tax is hidden through what the deceivers have termed inflation. The average citizen doesn't realize that they have been conned because inflation is actually a hidden tax. It has been reported that the average citizen lost $5,200 with inflation in 2022.[6]

Can you imagine how the average citizen would have reacted if "The Sheriff of Nottingham," aka the U.S. Congress had forcibly taken $5,200 directly from each American in order to fund their Ukraine War if we had been using the money of the Constitution – gold and silver? Remember, Ukraine is just one of their illegal wars. Using the money of the Constitution, "The Sheriff of Nottingham," aka the Congress would have been forced to take those exorbitant amounts of money directly from each American every time they waged one of their unconstitutional wars over the last one hundred years. Instead, the Congress has been using their paper "funny money" to tax us indirectly through inflation. Where's our modern-day Robin Hood when you need him the most?

I do not believe there is any way the American citizen would have stood for this kind of government theft and the burden that

---

[6]https://www.businessinsider.com/inflation-cost-americans-5200-extra-food-gas-energy-prices-bloomberg-2022-3?op=1

it has placed on the backs of the working class. When you view it in this way, it is easy to see why Washington warned that paper money would "***oppress the honest, and open the door to every species of fraud and injustice.***"

The positive thing to all of this, I guess, according to Ezekiel, is that the warmongers get to take their "weapons of war" with them "down to hell." (Ezekiel 32:5) I mean, who says that you can't take it with you?

Chapter 8
Save He That Had the Mark

"And that no man might buy or sell, save he that had the mark,"
Revelation 13:17

Our current monetary system, which began with the Legal Tenders Act of 1861 giving the federal government a pretext with which to print paper money was affirmed in *Knox*. It was then solidified in 1913 under the creation of the Federal Reserve and finalized by the Bretton Woods Agreement in 1944.

Under that Agreement, the world's currencies were unalterably pegged to the U.S. dollar. To the warmongers, everything was perfect with that arrangement except for one tiny, little problem. Their agreement also required that the paper dollar had to remain tied to a gold standard. Of course, this would not do for very long, because it was way too confining and restrictive. It's called a bait-and-switch. You know, get them to agree to something that seems reasonable, like keeping the paper dollar tied to gold, and then change the rules after everyone has signed on to the deal. Once you find yourself in a con, what can you do if they change the rules on you?

This is the real reason Nixon unilaterally cut all ties to gold in 1971. He knew no one would pull out of the deal, because they were already committed to the fraud. What, are they going to pull out over principle? Remember, we are dealing with politicians and bankers here. Of course, no one pulled out after Nixon changed the rules. The World Bank, the International Monetary Fund and Bank of International Settlements all stayed firmly in place keeping the U.S. paper dollar as the world's reserve currency. In simple terms, as the reserve currency this meant that no one in the world could buy or sell anything without the U.S. paper dollar.

Unfortunately, when it comes to the paper dollar, we have been acting much like the Jews who were living at the First Coming of Christ. You remember. When the Wise Men first arrived asking about the location of the Savior after following His star to Jerusalem, not one single person living in Jerusalem at the time, you know, the people who had been waiting for the Messiah for thousands of years, had any idea what the wise men were even talking about. Herod and "all Jerusalem" were totally clueless about an event that everyone in town would have been at least conceptually aware, for sure.

Here's the cold, hard truth. When looking to the fulfillment of prophecy, people have a tendency to focus on one particular detail which usually appeals to their carnal desires. We love blockbuster events. Events that are so obvious that everyone can see them happening. Unfortunately, those blockbuster ideas always obscure the important details behind the prophecy itself.

For example, the Jews wanted a huge event surrounding the arrival of their Messiah. They wanted their Messiah to come and destroy the Roman armies in a spectacular fashion and set the Jews free from their political captivity. They wanted a strong, invincible Messiah! This desire consumed them to the point that they couldn't focus on anything else. Even though the Jews studied the scriptures *"which are read every Sabbath day"* as the

Book of Acts tells us, still "they knew him not, nor yet the voices of the prophets." (Acts 13:27) (emphasis added). Do you really believe that it is going to be any different this time around?

To the spiritually alert, it should come as no surprise to learn that the First Coming of Christ was but a pattern for the much anticipated Second Coming. The Preacher explained it this way: *"That which hath been is now; and that which is to be hath already been; and God requireth that which is past."* (Eccl. 3:15) In other words, history repeats itself.

This theme is affirmed all throughout the scriptures. The Prophet Hosea explained it this way: "I have spoken by the prophets, and I have multiplied visions, and used similitudes, by the ministry of the prophets." (Hosea 12:10) "Similitudes" is the use of patterns which is a method that engages an ancient event or person to represent a yet future one.

Paul also discusses "the patterns of things" in Hebrews 8 and 9 that were used to help bring people to Christ—and, since God does not change His methods (i.e., He is the same yesterday, today and forever, Hebrews 13:8), we know that He will keep using patterns to reveal Himself and His work to His children. As such, this basically means that we are pretty much doomed to repeat the same mistakes as the first time around which is when the religious establishment pretty much got everything wrong about His arrival. They believed that their Messiah would come and destroy all of their enemies. They were so focused on this belief that they ignored everything else with respect to the prophecies. We are doing the same thing today.

When it comes to the prophecy pertaining to the Beast of Revelation and his mark, we have only been focused on one thing – a huge blockbuster event. We want to see a spectacular event in regard to the Beast and his mark – you know like world domination by an evil, maniacal force of globalists, where Nazi-like soldiers take control of everything and force us all to receive a computer chip under the skin, retinal scan, or some other kind of tracking device.

This is the story we have heard over and over again. Like the Jews, there is no attention to detail here by the ones pushing this narrative. There is no real identification of the mark or what Man is actually connected to the mark. If the "one world government" peddlers ever do get to the number of the Beast, they will go through so many different computations and algebraic expressions so as to boggle the mind and confuse anyone trying to understand what the heck they are even talking about. More importantly, with respect to their one world government extravaganza, that term is never used in the Book of Revelation, and it's not implied either. Of course, this will never stop a good ole one world government theorist from telling you all about it.

Ask anyone about the Book of Revelation, and they will only be able to talk about one other thing besides their one world government – they can't stop talking about the mark of the Beast. Yet, few, if any, can correlate their theory for the meaning of the mark with the rest of the prophecies corresponding to the Beast and his mark.

There are plenty of other prophecies relating to the Beast that need to correspond to the mark and its number or the theory is useless. When it comes to the mark and the number of the Beast, like the Jews, we have been ignoring those other prophecies to our detriment.

History is our Achilles' heel. Without it, we are unable to see the patterns and apply it to prophesy. Today's religious influencers will confine their interpretation to only one definition of the word mark. They tell us that the mark spoken of in the

Book of Revelation is a symbol, a name or other identifier such as a logo, a visible trace or impression such as a line, spot, number, letter, symbol, or tattoo. In light of this common definition, these influencers have very passionately pointed to physical markers like computer chips as fulfillment of the mark.

However, as you might have come to expect by now, there is another more relevant definition of the word mark from a historical perspective that is rarely, if ever, brought up by those influencers. The word mark can also refer to a country's currency. For example, the mark was used in Germany, Scotland, and it was also used to define the value of the official gold and silver currencies of the Holy Roman Empire.

Now this bit of information should not come as a surprise given our prior, extensive discussion on the history of currency in the United States. Once the correct interpretation of the word is understood, the prophecy takes on a whole new meaning: *"And that no man might buy or sell, save he that had the mark [currency] of the beast..." (emphasis added) (Rev. 13:17)*

This definition when read this way makes much more sense than some silly tattoo or a computer chip. More importantly, we can now understand why Delegate George Read spoke about the mark of the Beast when the Convention was debating the issue of paper currency. He obviously understood the correct interpretation of the word and somehow knew what its use here in the United States would mean. The mark of the Beast is the ***currency*** of the Beast. It should not be interpreted as a line, spot, number, letter, symbol, tattoo, or computer chip of the Beast.

Chapter 9
For It Is the Number of a Man

*"Here is wisdom, Let him that hath understanding count the number of the Beast: **for it is the number of a man.**"*
Revelation 13:18

Now that we have established a much more credible alternative to the meaning behind the Mark of the Beast, we need to analyze all of the other corresponding prophecies related to the Beast to see if this interpretation really is accurate and if the U.S. paper dollar applies.

One of the most common corresponding prophecies associated with the Mark of the Beast is the Beast's number. The prophecy instructs us to "count the number of the beast: for it is the number of a man; and his number is Six hundred threescore and six." Rev. 13:18. Remember, if Delegate Read's analysis is correct, then we should be looking for a paper currency that has a number that is associated with a specific man and that number is six hundred threescore and six.

This is very simple and straightforward, and, once again, as you might expect, history will serve to illuminate a new and more plausible meaning behind the Beast's number. According to the dictionary, score means twenty. Therefore, three score is three times twenty which equals sixty. The prophecy, therefore, reads that the number of the Beast is six hundred sixty and six. Let me be clear. It is not written as 666. It is written out to read six hundred sixty and six. What's the difference? Well, history will teach us that the number 666 is the Arabic way of writing six hundred sixty and six. Everyone in the Christian world thinks only about the Arabic way of writing the number – 666 – because that is our frame of reference.

The European Arabic numeral system, which uses 10 digits from zero to nine did not come in common use until the twelfth century. The writer of the book of Revelation was a man known as John the Revelator who was banned to the Isle of Patmos by the Roman government around 95 AD, almost one thousand and two hundred years before the Arabic writing system became vogue in the Western world. In order to understand John's writings, we first need to understand his frame of reference.

For some reason, no one has ever really talked about this very important fact. We should understand what John's point of reference was if we're going to understand the number of the Beast. He lived under the influence of the Roman Empire. This meant that the Roman way of doing things would obviously have an impact on the way John viewed the world. As most of us know, the Romans did not write numbers the way we do now. Its writing system was definitely NOT the Arabic writing system. This is an extremely important distinction.

Before trying to figure out the number of the Mark of the Beast, we should really try and think about Roman influence. John's frame of reference was not the Arabic writing system that produced the popular label of 666, because that writing system did not even exist at the time. It didn't exist for nearly one thousand and two hundred years after John received his revelation. Also, remember that the scripture clearly says that it is the number of a man. Here's where it gets interesting. Stop and pull out a paper dollar and look at it like it was the first time you've ever seen it. Think about the number of the Mark of the Beast in that context. You should now be able to see something that you've never seen before given our historical analysis of the paper dollar. The man George Washington is the face of the paper dollar. The man George Washington personifies the dollar bill in every aspect. You see that, right?

Now, look where his name is written on the paper dollar and the two letters that are inseparably connected to his name. Everyone knows it. Everyone sees it every single day, but no one ever gives it a second thought, because it is hiding in plain sight. Yet, there it is in big, bold **Roman numerals** just like it would have been when John saw it. Go ahead, look for yourself. His name is written next to his portrait as Washington, **DC**. It is always there. It doesn't change, and it is right next to the picture of the man – George Washington. Since John was subject to Roman influence and given the fact that the back of the dollar also uses Roman letters, it is extremely reasonable to suppose that the "DC" that is always written next to Washington's name on the unconstitutional paper dollar would have been viewed by the writer of the Book of Revelation as the Roman Number DC or Six Hundred.

This was clearly John's frame of reference, and it goes to reason that his writings would have reflected the same. Think of it this way. When Elijah was taken up into Heaven, the scripture tells us that he was taken up into Heaven in a "chariot of fire." The chariot was their frame of reference for travel, so they described the flying machine that carried Elijah away as a *chariot.* They had no other reference for a flying machine in which people could travel, so they called it a chariot. This particular chariot was unlike anything they had ever seen, but how else would they have described it?

The writer did try and distinguish this particular chariot by telling us that it was a chariot of fire. Without a doubt, the Spirit could have given the modern name for the machine, but the writer used his frame of reference instead as is the case with all of the writers in the Bible when recording their prophecies. Their mode of transportation was the chariot, which is why the writer used the name chariot, and he could see that fire was associated with the chariot that had been sent to retrieve Elijah.

This is clearly the case with John and his system of writing. He was not familiar with the Arabic style of writing and conceptually would not even have understood the Arabic number 666, because he had no frame of reference. Yet, clearly, he would have recognized the letters DC and his frame of reference would have interpreted the DC as the number six hundred—not the Arabic 600.

Clearly, the number "DC" is always associated with the man George Washington – always. I guess you could say that it was his number. Now, I know what you are thinking – what about the last part of the number? You know, the sixty and sixth part. Simple. Washington retired from public life at the end of his 66th year, and John would have been shown this fact, since he mentions it.

George Washington left Washington, DC when he was sixty and six. So, the number of the man George Washington is clearly Six Hundred Sixty and Six. His name is always associated with the Roman letters DC, and when Washington was no longer a part of DC, he left at Sixty and Six years of age. See. No acrobats. No computations or algebraic expressions needed. It is really that simple. The man and his number are the only thing associated inseparably with the unconstitutional mark/currency also known as the U.S. paper dollar just as Delegate Read warned us about over two hundred years ago. John tells us, "Here is wisdom. Let him that hath understanding count the number of the beast." (Rev. 13:18) Wisdom is needed in order to decipher John's mysteries. I would venture to guess that very few if any of the one world government/666 theorists have used the wisdom described herein to arrive at their conclusions.

Those religious leaders and influencers who would have you believe that the number is the Arabic 666 and that it will be found on either a patent, a Congressional House bill, or a computer chip are the same leaders that Isaiah warned about – "the leaders of this people cause them to err." (Is. 9:16). Don't fall for it.

Their computer chips, their patents and their Congressional House bills do not have anything to do with the number of a man nor the context from which John was living nor the buying and selling of goods and services as does the currency of the United States nor are they tied back to anything as compelling as the history of the paper dollar as described herein.

Besides, the numbers your uninspired leaders have been giving you are connected to patents, legislation and/or computers – NOT a man. Yet, every time you look at the U.S. mark/currency, it indisputably shows the picture of a man named Washington with his name Washington written next to his picture followed by the letters DC which is the Roman numeral for 600 and all the world's financial transactions have to use the U.S. paper dollar. Nothing could be more simple to see and describe, but it requires a little bit of wisdom to understand it. Admittedly, cognitive dissonance is a powerful thing to overcome. Remember Occam's razor? All of the other efforts made to describe John's prophecy are anything but simple or easy to see or understand except this one.

As we all know, from our point of reference, the letters DC stands for the District of Columbia, which the entire world knows is the seat of power for the United States. The place that bears the name of Washington and the place that he founded and for which he gave his entire life. Therefore, when he finally retired and left DC for good at sixty and six years of age, it is easy to see how John would have connected the age of the man to DC. It's not a coincidence. It has been hiding in plain sight for anyone "that hath understanding" to see.

The scripture very clearly points out that it is the "number of his name." (Rev. 13:17). His name is the number or, rather, the number is in his name. Washington's name is always accompanied by DC and implicitly contains the additional number sixty and six, because that's when he left the seat of power that is DC. It is the name everyone uses when referring to that seat of power in the United States – Washington (who was sixty and six when he left) DC.

This is a corresponding prophecy that needs to be considered in conjunction with any theory of the mark of the beast. I've yet to see any that fits like this one does. It is not enough just to say that a computer chip owned and controlled by a one world government fulfills the prophecy, and that the chip is the mark of the beast. The chip needs to be rationally tied to the number six hundred sixty and six and that number needs to be tied to the name of a man, and it needs to be tied directly to a mark/currency because the mark is the mechanism with which to buy and sell. It can't be a patent. It can't be a Congressional House bill with too many 6's in its title.

In all the years, I've been following their theories in this regard, no one has yet been able to tie this prophecy, as it is written, directly to their theories. In fact, they never even seem to be concerned with making any of these connections at all. It's always one world government, computer chip, and we'll figure the rest out later kind of a thing. It's as if they are so focused on making their case for a one world government with their computer chips that nothing else matters.

Chapter 10
Who Is Able to Make War with Him?

"Who is like unto the beast? Who is able to make war with him?"
Revelation 13:17

As previously discussed, it is important to reiterate that the one world government theory does not fulfill any of the other corresponding prophecies associated with the mark of the Beast. The individuals who promote their different ideas on the meaning of the mark rarely delve into the rest of the corresponding prophecies associated with the Beast.

They only focus on the number "666" and then they jump right off into one world government from there. This is sloppy reasoning at best. They also never really identify the specific prophecy that actually predicts a one world government. To these individuals, nothing else matters but their 666, their computer chips and their Nazi-esque one world government. They are just like the Jews at Christ's First Coming who would only focus on one theme and one theme only – their Messiah was going to come and destroy all His enemies and establish His throne. The Jews ignored the rest of the prophecies and patterns along with any and all contradictions because they were obsessed.

The rest of this work illustrates how the remaining prophecies pertaining to the Beast continue to correspond directly to the corrupt United States government and its unconstitutional mark/currency – the U.S. paper dollar. There will be no bootstrapping either in making the rest of the corresponding prophecies fit as you will see.

The next one of the corresponding prophecies that we are going to cover concerns war and the Beast's ability to wage it. Our historical deficit concerning our paper money's history has led us into a kind of financial bondage instigated by the warmongers, where our net incomes and savings fall drastically behind inflation and the inability of our paper currency to hold its value.

These warmongers are the same individuals Eisenhower warned us about, even though no one has ever wanted to heed the warning and confront these murderers. He referred to them as the Military Industrial Complex. Unfortunately, we as a nation have been unable to free ourselves from the killing machine that is the Military Industrial Complex (hereinafter referred to as "MIC") for over one hundred years.

It is imperative to realize that none of the killing would have even been possible without the paper dollar. The warmongers inside MIC have been able to print limitless quantities of money with the paper dollar in order to fund their endless wars, while simultaneously destroying the working man's savings and wages with their hidden tax otherwise known as inflation and the dollar's devaluation. Every so often, someone comes along who starts shouting about balanced budgets and deficit spending, but they are only attacking the symptoms of the real problem. Every problem we have experienced as a nation can be traced back to one thing – love for the paper dollar… you remember, just like Paul said.

Ever since the Legal Tenders Act of 1861 and the decision in *Knox*, it is indisputable that an unending stream of wars have been poured out upon the world. It started with the Civil War and then went on to include the Spanish-American War, World Wars I and II, the Korean War, the Vietnam War, the Bay of Pigs, the Invasion of Grenada and Panama, the Persian Gulf War, Bosnia, the twenty-year war in Afghanistan, Iraq, Somalia and Kenya, Operation Ocean Shield in the Indian Ocean, Libya, Uganda, Syria, Yemeni, and now Ukraine.

There literally has been no peace since we cast the Constitution aside with the *Knox* decision in favor of a worthless paper dollar. We could have avoided those wars, death and tragedy had we just listened to the Framers of the Constitution and followed it.

The fact is, our world is a very, very dangerous place because of arrogance and a disregard for the Framers. Just look at what their warmonger policies have done to us and the rest of the world. We created and used the nuclear bomb, so now we have to be the ones to protect the world from the nuclear bomb. We created the modern war machine, so now we have to be the ones to protect the world from that war machine by selling our wares to our "allies."

We've destabilized the world through our war-driven, interventionist, regime-change policies, so now we have to protect the world from the bad guys created by the chaos used for regime change. You know, we have to destroy the bad governments so we can save them from themselves. All these same arguments are once again being rehashed in order to legitimize another endless war in the Ukraine. The difference there, of course, is that Ukraine is not actually an ally but that's ok because we didn't sell our wares to Ukraine. We just gave it to them.

The Beast's ability to make war is the next corresponding prophecy that needs to be considered in conjunction with the mark of the Beast. According to the prophecy, we read that no one is able to make war with the Beast – "Who is like unto the beast? Who is able to make war with him?" (Rev. 13:4) In other words, the Beast is so powerful everyone realizes that no one can make war with him. Clearly, the Beast is the most powerful military nation in the world according to this prophecy.

How does the U.S. square with this prediction you ask? Seriously? No one can deny that the U.S. has been the most powerful nation that has ever existed on the face of the earth with a military prowess unrivalled by anyone. There has been no other nation in the entire history of the world that has been as powerful as the U.S. military. No one. You know that, right?

For those who buy into the one world government theory, if the war prophecy did apply to a one world government, how would it make any sense? If there is a one world government, that would mean by default that there are no other governments in the world. You know, because it is a one world government, which means one government only. If there are no other governments, why would anyone even ask the question, "Who is like unto the beast? Who is able to make war with him?" since there is no other government left in the world with which to even challenge it and to make war against it?

Obviously, this prophecy can't be referring to a one world government for if there is only one government why would anyone ask who can make war with itself? To the rational, unbiased mind, it is clear that the prophecy implies the existence of more than one nation. This is the reason the other nations are asking the question – who can make war with the nation that is the Beast?

Chapter 11
Seven Heads and Ten Horns

"And I stood upon the sand of the sea, and saw a beast rise up out of the sea, having seven heads and ten horns."
Revelation 13:1

Another important prophecy relating to the Beast concerns its geography. We learn from the scriptures that the Beast most definitely will not be coming out of continental Europe or even Asia for that matter. Most theories seem to promote the idea that the Beast will be coming from that part of the world but the prophecy contradicts this assumption.

It specifically says that the Beast will rise up out of the sea—by default that means it is NOT rising up out of a continent—"I stood upon the sand of the sea, and saw a beast rise up out of the sea." (Rev. 13:1). How is this description confusing – the sea versus Continental Europe/Asia? You have to use some serious bootstrapping to even try to make that argument, but as I've said the influencers peddling the "666" tattoo/computer chip theory don't seem to be interested in consistency. They fantasize about their big, bad one world Nazi-esque government running around the globe forcibly marking people with a "666" tattoo and jamming a computer chip under their skin.

Yet, to the open-minded individual, it is easy to recognize that the Beast must rise up out of the sea and not up out of the continental governments of the Old World. The United States is smack dab in the middle of the sea... You know, because we have the Atlantic Ocean on one side and the Pacific on the other.

Prior to World War II, we did not have the prominence that we do now. We rose up out of the Pacific and Atlantic Oceans with all the world watching following the end of World War II to become *the most powerful nation on the earth.* Even before it happened, Hamilton spoke of it when arguing that the continental "powers of Europe" were doing everything aimed at "clipping the wings by which we might soar to a dangerous greatness." Hamilton, The Federalist Papers, Ltr. 11, 2.

He understood that our country was destined for greatness so much so that it would be dangerous to the established order of the Old World and that only the Constitution could facilitate that rise, and rise we have, up out of the sea following the great World Wars only to fall prey to corrupt and conspiring politicians, bureaucrats and military contractors.

During World War II, we gained access to nuclear weapons; we created the Military Industrial Complex, but most significantly we became the most powerful nation in the history of the world. At that point, we became an entirely different nation than we were in our humble beginnings. We lost our innocence so-to-speak by changing all the rules laid down by the Founders. Everything our Founders held dear, we turned away from to forge our own set of guidelines.

The first rule our leaders broke was the **Great Rule** laid down by George Washington in his Farewell Address. If there is one thing that Washington and the Framers agreed upon, it was the danger that comes with foreign alliances. This subject was so important that Washington used his Farewell Address to denounce the formation of these kinds of alliances. "It is our true policy," Washington explained, "to steer clear of permanent alliances with any portion of the foreign world;" Washington's Farewell Address.

This code of conduct is what Washington referred to as the **Great Rule** – "The **great rule** of conduct for us in regard to foreign nations is in extending our commercial relations, to have with them *as little political connection as possible*." Id. (emphasis added) He warned us that foreign influence is the enemy of Republican government: "Against the insidious wiles of foreign influence (I conjure you to believe me, fellow-citizens) the jealousy of a free people ought to be constantly awake, since history and experience prove that *foreign influence is one of the most baneful foes of republican government*." Id.

Hamilton also highlighted foreign influence as a detriment to Republican governments – "One of the weak sides of republics, among their numerous advantages, is that they afford too easy an inlet to foreign corruption." Hamilton, The Federalist Papers, Ltr. 22, 12.

By adhering to the Great Rule, Washington promised that we would have complete freedom over our own destiny by avoiding entanglements with the Old World. The Great Rule was reaffirmed by John Quincy Adams who expounded it to mean that we as a nation "go not abroad in search of monsters to destroy." To do so, he warned, would make us the "dictatress of the world" a condition in which we now find ourselves.

Tragically, entangling alliances have become the norm with our corrupt politicians. They make the argument that the world is such a dangerous place that we must be everywhere and be all things to everyone in order to keep it safe. They actually disparage the Framers, calling them Isolationists, which apparently is a really bad thing. These politicians believe that they are a lot smarter than our Founding Fathers. Our know-it-all politicians had to discard the Great Rule in order to engage in their endless wars. They told us these endless wars were needed so that we could have peace in the world.

Sadly, the very thing decried by our First Great President has now become the obsession of our politicians. How much of our wealth has been lost through the transfers of trillions of dollars to the Military Industrial Complex and foreign governments? How many lives have been lost fighting in their wars? How much of our own personal quests and desires have been crushed by the dictates of the warmongers' agenda?

While the Great Rule was adhered to by our early leaders, since Congress started printing paper money, our modern leaders have been going abroad in search of monsters to destroy for a long time. This dangerous policy has spread our influence throughout the world until we have created a military presence that rivals any prior empire.

We tell ourselves that we are the "good guys" in order to justify our unwinding of the Great Rule, but we have killed far too many children, women and men in our quest to destroy the monsters for that argument to hold water. We have become so delusional in this apostate policy that we even justify all the killing. Remember the public interview with Madame Albright wherein she said that the war they waged in the Middle East that caused the death of nearly **one million children** was "worth it"? Now, couple that number with the lives of the babies we've taken through abortion in this country, so any attempt to refer to us as the "good guys" is simply not tenable.

I'm reminded of the verse in Matthew wherein the Lord warns that "whoso shall offend one of these little ones which believe in me it were better for him that a millstone were hanged about his neck, and that he were drowned in the depth of the sea." Matt. 18:6

Believing the Great Rule to be outdated, our politicians have formed a number of permanent alliances. It is impossible to maintain any permanent alliance without putting our Constitutional Republic in jeopardy. To the unbiased spectator, it should be painfully obvious that the defenders of today's modern alliances are more interested in maintaining their warmongering views than they are in defending the U.S. Constitution.

The best proof of this is the NATO alliance. Under the NATO treaty, there is a very dangerous provision otherwise known as Article V. Under that Article, it requires us to go to war if any member of the alliance is attacked. It declares that an attack upon any member of NATO is an attack upon the whole. The net effect of this provision is to completely nullify Article I, §8, cl.11 of the U.S. Constitution, which exclusively places the power to declare war in the hands of Congress.

Article V of the NATO treaty also destroys the Supremacy Clause of the U.S. Constitution by making it subservient to the NATO treaty. Congress will have no say as to whether or not we go to war if Article V of the NATO treaty is invoked. By surrendering its authority under Article V, Congress has ceded its authority to control war over to the warmongers that is the Military Industrial Complex. This is one of the main reasons we have become so proficient at war-making. The U.S. has definitely fulfilled the prophecy that no one is able to make war with us.

Another important part of the prophecy wherein John reports seeing the Beast rising up out of the sea is the physical description of the Beast. The Beast has seven heads and ten horns – "I… saw a beast rise up out of the sea, having seven heads and ten horns." (Rev. 13:1). Before your mind runs wild with extraterrestrial visions of grandeur, John explains in another chapter that the seven heads and ten horns are symbolic. They represent "seven kings... and ten kings." (Rev. 17:10,12) In other words, the Beast, which is a nation that rises up out of the sea does not act alone and is not a one world government. If so, there couldn't be at least two other groups of seven and ten kings affiliated with it.

Of course, the influencers won't be able to help themselves from trying to bootstrap this thing and claim that the seven and ten are not really sovereign but are more like governors rather than kings who have been given their little section of earth that the Beast gives them to govern. Yet, if that were the case, John would have referred to them as governors and not kings. The word king intrinsically implies a sovereign nation ruled by its own ruler.

On the other hand, once again, using Occam's razor as our guide, and we just accept the simple wording of the prophecy, we merely have to look around to see if the U.S. fits John's seven and ten description. When we do, we of course will see that the description easily fits. The U.S. has been part of an organization known as the G-7 (Group of Seven) since 1976. The seven nations included in this international group are known as the seven most industrialized nations in the world. Russia joined the Group in 1998 making it the G-8 but was kicked out in 2014 after it annexed Crimea. (The number 8, just so you know, is also mentioned in Revelation chapter 17 verse 11.) The finance ministers of the G-7 meet at least annually to discuss key issues related to global economic stability. Look at that! It's all about the money again.

Next, as you would expect, there is another group that includes the number ten. The G-10 or Group of Ten nations also meet regularly to handle issues related to the IMF (the International Monetary Fund) and the BIS (the Bank of International Settlements). In other words, the G-7 basically sets economic policy, and the G-10 implements it through the IMF and the BIS. In case you missed it, this all has to do with the U.S. paper dollar bill. Every financial transaction in the world has to be converted into dollars through the BIS. In other words, no one can buy or sell without it.

There's another corresponding prophecy respecting these two groups that needs to fit with the United States as well if we are to remain consistent in our application. We learn from the scripture that one of the seven heads is "wounded to death," but the "deadly wound is healed." Remember, John identifies these seven heads as kingdoms. Perhaps you are wondering which country of the G-7 fits that description for us to stay consistent?

At the end of World War II, one of the G-7 countries was not only defeated, but it was destroyed. It was split in half, and for all intents and purposes became a dead nation. There was no more nation of Germany. It was gone. It died. Where we had one united, powerful Nation of Germany, it became two separate entities after it died from the wounds inflicted on it by the allied powers.

Now, go back and look at the news headlines when the Berlin Wall finally fell, and Germany became a nation once again. It was described as a miracle – **"Many call it a miracle, Germany's peaceful revolution in 1989 and reunification less than a year later."**[7] Germany's deadly wound from World War

---

[7] https://www.bbc.com/news/world-europe-11447587

II was finally healed unexpectedly, and Germany became a country once again.

Another corresponding prophecy tells us that the Beast can actually call down fire from Heaven for all the world to see – "and he doeth great wonders, so that he maketh fire come down from heaven on the earth in the sight of all men." (Rev. 13:13). So, I know right off, you are skeptical again. You are thinking Hollywood. You know, Independence Day where the invading aliens send a large beam of fire down onto the White House. That's the kind of fire coming down from Heaven that you are thinking about, right? Well, step back for a moment and put your common sense hat back on and look around for a minute.

What has the U.S. done that easily supports the veracity of this prophecy? What person is there on the earth who has not seen the fire that dropped from the sky over Hiroshima and Nagasaki with its ensuing, hellish, fiery mushroom cloud? Who does not recognize the power of that image and the ensuing fear that fills the hearts of everyone who sees it, and what it must have looked like to John two thousand years ago?

It most definitely looked like fire coming down from the Heavens after being dropped from a flying machine. John doesn't say a beam of fire, your imagination did. John says the Beast makes "fire come down from Heaven," which can easily be interpreted as being dropped down from the skies from an airplane.

Lest anyone misunderstand, this discussion is not an attack upon the Constitutional Republic of the United States nor upon the few good Patriots left. This is an attack upon the usurpers and what they have turned us into.

The Constitution was never the problem. All of our problems have resulted from ignoring and usurping the Constitution and allowing our politicians to act outside the Constitution, thereby forcing us back to the Old World and all of its old, despotic, disastrous practices.

Like Isaiah said, "This people draw near to me with their mouth, and with their lips do honor me, but have removed their heart far from me." (Is. 29:13) We too give lip service to our Constitution, but as The Federalist Papers clearly show, we have long abandoned the Constitutional Republic they gave us. We have morphed into a hedonistic, factious democracy that has been funded and fueled entirely by the rage for paper money.

Incidentally, according to Madison, democracies always die violent deaths or morph into tyrannical governments. Madison, The Federalist Papers, Ltr. 10. It's kind of hard to miss the anger, division and contention that is so pervasive in our democratic nation today.

Rest assured, these attitudes will continue to spill into more and more violence until the government moves in to crush the violent factions, and in so doing, they will also have to crush everyone's liberties in the process. The Republic is gone.

Chapter 12
And All the World Wondered after the Beast

"And all the world wondered after the beast, and they worshipped the dragon which gave power unto the beast: and they worshipped the Beast..."
Revelation 13:3-4

The next corresponding prophecy that needs to be considered in conjunction with the Beast puts another stake in the heart of the one world government theorists. John tells us that the Beast is wonderful, so much so that the entire world seems enamored by it. However, according to the one world government theory, the Beast is a dark, Nazi-esque entity that uses harsh and foreboding tactics to force people to do the bidding of the one world government.

This tactic, of course, is what Satan wants you to think. Remember, Satan is a con man. He likes to entice people to his way of doing things. He doesn't like to force people to his side of the tracks. He knows that it is far easier to attract bees with honey than it is with vinegar. He is also very good at gaslighting and distracting. He can transform himself unto an angel of light, remember? (2 Cor. 11:14)

Satan wants you to believe that the Beast is extremely dark, so much so, that when it does show up, it will be easily recognizable. You know – because it will be so dark and so evil. While everyone is distracted with this Hollywood version of the Beast, Satan knows that no one will notice the real Beast, because everyone is so completely infatuated with it. Like always, Satan gets us hooked with his deceptions and distractions, and nobody is the wiser.

Listen to John's description. He tells us that "all the world **wondered** after the beast." (emphasis added) Enamored by its presence, the world also ponders the question, "Who is like unto the beast?" (Rev. 13:4) In other words, who is its equal? The Beast is unlike anything the world has ever known. We are awed by it. We are enamored with it. We love it!

Think about the definition of the word wondered. When we wonder after something, the dictionary tells us that it means we are consumed with "rapt attention" or "amazed admiration." Does this definition fit the one world government theory even remotely? You know – the one where everyone is forced by the WEF's Klaus Schwab to take his computer chip and mandatory vaccine so that we can all be under his constant surveillance forever?

Seriously? Who is going to be enamored by those kinds of tactics except, maybe, for a few nut jobs? All the talk about Klaus Schwab and his Great Reset plans – "you'll own nothing and be happy" – has most definitely created paranoia and resentment among large groups of people. It has not created wonder or amazed admiration or rapt attention as the prophecy predicts.

If Klaus Schwab's vision for the future fulfills that prophecy, why are so many of us still so skeptical and determined not to take marching orders from Klaus or his WEF henchmen or henchwomen? Remember, it has to be the "whole world" for the prophecy to fit. I would venture to guess that most are definitely not in "rapt attention" nor in "amazed admiration" with Klaus and his psychotic sidekicks such as Yuval Noah Harari. If there ever was an Antichrist, Harari would be it with all of his blasphemous speech about fairytales and the Resurrection of Christ. Most of us, I think, would like to see that godless group removed from the scene entirely. Clearly, no one is wondering after them in the least.

If it's not the Klaus Schwab one world government that fits the description of all the world wondering after it, then which country does induce the whole world to fawn in wonder and amazement? Gee, now let me think… Oh, yes, the nation that the entire world is now flooding to and illegally crossing its borders.

Unfortunately, too many of us, much like the Jews in Christ's day, are still waiting for someone or something else to appear on the scene because we already have our minds made up. You know, we want something that fits more along the lines of Hollywood's description of the Beast. I assure you that Hollywood's description is wrong and is part of Satan's deception.

This should come as no big surprise, however, since Hollywood is saturated with perverts and pedophiles. How could that group of deviants be inspired enough to telegraph the identity of the prophetic Beast from scripture? I think not.

The open-minded, rational, critically thinking individual will be able see the world as it truly exists. Who will seriously try and deny the fact that there has never been, in the history of the entire world, a nation "like unto the" United States? Who will seriously try and deny that the entire world has not, at one time or another, been infatuated with the United States? Who will seriously try and deny that basically everyone (and their mother) wants to be here? Who will seriously try and deny that pretty much everyone in the world is filled with "rapt attention" and "amazed admiration" for the United States?

I don't care how much we romanticize about the Roman Empire, the Greeks, the Chinese Dynasties, or the British Empire, they ALL pale in comparison to the United States with all of its wealth, power and influence and its undeniable allure. Not only is it the most powerful nation ever in the history of the world, so much so that no one can wage war against us, it is literally the richest nation ever to have existed on the planet. It is no doubt that the entire world wonders after the United States with envy. This obvious fact should come as no surprise to anyone. Yet, no one has been able to connect the dots and that is because of the infatuation.

Who in their wildest dreams living in the Roman or British Empires could ever have imagined a time when every single citizen has a car to drive around, when everyone has a television, a computer, an iPhone, and enough food to make us the fattest nation on earth? As an aside, one could make the argument that Isaiah had the fall of the United States in mind when he noted that "the waste places of the fat ones shall strangers eat" (Is. 5:17), but I digress.

All of our wealth and power has truly made us the envy of the world, so that the entire world does want to be here. Are we seriously going to ignore all of the evidence staring us in the face because we're still waiting for another empire to rise up that can top all of the credentials of the United States? Let's see now – who does that remind me of? Oh, yes! The ones who are still waiting for their Messiah, while choosing to ignore the reality of

Jesus, the prophecies, and the sacrificial rites of the Law of Moses that clearly pointed to the sacrifice of Jesus.

Of course, if we're still not convinced, then good luck with that evil one world government empire. I'm sure it's going to be really, really evil – just the way we like it because Hollywood has conditioned us so well. They love telegraphing to the audience through predictive programming and highlighting the bad guys with those uniforms. That way, when Klaus Schwab and his minions do come for us with their blue helmets and one world government tyranny, we will be able to know that they are working for the Beast. This way, we can be really, really brave and refuse to have anything to do with them just like we've always imagined in our minds that we would. You know – just like we did during the Covid lockdowns with all of those unconstitutional mandates – well, some of us, anyway.

This kind of thinking always reminds me of Paul's prophecy that "the time will come when they will not endure sound doctrine… and they shall turn away from the truth, and shall be turned unto fables." (2 Tim. 4:3-4) Sound familiar?

Hollywood is a land of fairytales. Think about it. When the bulk of our spare time is spent watching only movies and television instead of also studying the scriptures and our founding documents, how exactly will we be able to distinguish between truth and fairytales? Klaus Schwab is a distraction. The United States clearly fulfills the prophecy in this regard and the prophecies we've discussed in prior chapters.

Chapter 13
A Woman upon a Scarlet Colored Beast Having Seven Heads and Ten Horns

> *"And I saw a woman sit upon a scarlet colored beast, full of names of blasphemy, having seven heads and ten horns… And in her was found the blood of prophets, and of saints, and of all that were slain upon the earth."*
> Revelation 17:3; 18:24.

In order to understand the next corresponding prophecy, we need to reach back into our nation's history once again to lay the groundwork. There is another part of history about the Civil War which I am sure you never read about in history class. This bit of history will not go over well with the status quo, I am sure. In fact, when I have discussed it in certain circles with others myself, it has never been well received, but it is there, nonetheless. There is no denying it. It is a fact.

Were you aware that following the end of the Civil War the United States severed all diplomatic ties with the Vatican? Are you surprised? Very few U.S. citizens even know about this history and the reason for it. It will also most likely surprise you to learn that the reason for the diplomatic severance with Rome was because there were many in and out of government who believed at the time that the Pope through the use of an organization known as the Jesuits was the real culprit behind the assassination of President Lincoln. Yeah, this bit of history is not too popular any more. I have been accused of being anti-Catholic in my historical discussions of the matter.

My detractors finally just dismissed the matter for its "frivolous nature." Apparently, those men who sacrificed so much to win the Civil War were frivolous bigots. The members of today's status quo are so much more enlightened, don't you think? After all, the status quo has sacrificed and given so much for our country, wouldn't you agree?

One hero of the Civil War did write about it, though. His name was General Thomas Maley Harris, MD who authored his thesis for the argument in 1897 with his book *Rome's Responsibility for the Assassination of Abraham Lincoln*. In the book's introduction, General Harris writes that "the reader of this little book will see that we have ample reasons for making this charge" and then goes on to make the case for the assassination with witnesses and the like. What is even more fascinating to me is the fact that diplomatic ties were not restored until over 100 years later.

It was Ronald Reagan in 1984 who finally restored those diplomatic relations which were terminated in 1867. What intrigues me even more is the historical fact that ever since those diplomatic ties were renewed, we have watched every U.S. President travel to the Vatican to "kiss the ring."

Critically thinking individuals should be able to recognize that, if the U.S. were actually in control of its own destiny and not beholden to more sinister organizations, it would make more sense for the Pope to come here to visit the U.S. president – not the other way around. On its face, these visits have appeared to be more of a summons to Rome than something in the ordinary course of diplomatic visitations. I am not alone in this thinking.

According to one author, "The Jesuit oaths are blood-curdling, being in fact the 'cult of death,' always seeking to poison the innocent minds of the young with pernicious Jesuit ideologies such as Communism, Fascism, Feminism, Scientism, Helio-centrism, Evolution, and Atheism. They are responsible for every war, revolution, and political assassination in the last five hundred years as they attempt to destroy any obstacle to Rome's ascendency and dominion through its NWO." (emphasis added.) [8]

The claim has also been made that the "Jesuits control all world banking" and that "There is no military force they can't co-opt and using the U.S. military, NATO, the IDF, and Blackwater they enforce Rome's edicts without mercy, daily, anywhere in the world today just as Imperial Rome did two thousand years ago." *Id.*

Finally, the claim has been made by the above author that the Pope, through the Jesuits act "as administrators of the papal inquisitions which began in the twelfth century and have continued right up to the present time murdering countless millions of people worldwide." *Id.*

The purpose of my series on *The U.S. Paper Dollar* is not to detail all the excesses of the Pope and the Jesuits. The dark and maniacal deeds of the Middle Ages are well known and documented, but the continuation of those excesses into the present day are not so well publicized.

---

[8] http://www.darknessisfalling.com/darknessisfallingblogblog/the-jesuits-unholy-order-of-evil; https://www.jamesjpn.net/protestant-authors/the-jesuits-unholy-order-of-evil/

One of the reasons for this phenomenon was described by Civil War General Harris in his book back in 1897, "By the skillful use of her almost boundless wealth, Rome has secured control of the public press, and can put before the American people just what she chooses and can withhold from them whatever she chooses to suppress." Sound familiar? It was the press back then, but it is the mainstream media and the social tech giants today that keep so many of us in ignorance.

I know that it's not pleasant to think or talk of such things, but the fact remains, the Papacy has a sordid, bloody and perverted past, which appears to have forged right on into the present time at least according to some. It is no secret that our Forefathers fled Europe to escape the tyranny of the Pope and the Crown, but according to many at the time of the Civil War, like General Harris, that tyranny followed us to our shores and had its hand on certain levers of power.

If these claims are true, we have been carrying the monetary and international policies of the Papacy on our backs with the paper dollar in order to wage war and wreak financial devastation on the masses. The U.S. with its military might and paper dollar sustains and maintains the power and control of the Pope throughout the world, but it is not a unification of governments. It is a partnership. The one world government theory has been used to deceive you. It has been promoted to keep you from seeing what is really happening.

Like John Adams said, "Facts are stubborn things," and there's this annoying little chapter in the Book of Revelation that once again debunks the one world government version of the story that Hollywood loves to promote. In Chapter 18 of the Book of Revelation, we learn the most important thing about the partnership that exists between the Whore of Babylon and the 7-

headed 10-horned Beast that carries her. According to Shaun Casey, a professor in Georgetown University's Walsh School of Foreign Service, we are in a partnership with the Vatican – "I think they discovered in Pope Francis a very willing partner to address some of these massive global issues like climate change, like refugees."[9]

In Chapter 18, we find out who laments the most over the destruction of the Whore of Babylon and the Beast. The answer is going to surprise you. I'm warning you. The only ones "weeping and wailing" about the fall of the Whore of Babylon and the Beast are not the dark soldiers of some world government tyrannical regime nor is it the legions of bureaucrats that would be needed to run such an organization.

No, it is the mild-mannered "merchants" (v.15) of the world. Yes, you heard me. It is the "merchants" who are all torn up about the fall of the Beast and its Whore. I know, it's not very insidious, but it's the truth. It is the merchants who are making all the fuss. If you understood how the paper dollar works, it wouldn't surprise you, though, since in this paper dollar driven economy, the merchants are the ones who are "made rich." (v.19)

I know you were expecting it to be the armies of the beasts and all of those evil looking, helmet-clad soldiers and their bureaucratic counterparts who should be the ones most upset about losing their power at the fall of the Beast and the Whore. Admit it. You were thinking that the ones who are stationed everywhere across the globe in the one world government version of the Beast in order to keep the masses in check would be the most upset about losing their control over the masses. You know, it's supposed to be the ones with their sophisticated

---

[9] https://www.npr.org/2021/10/29/1050332844/a-look-back-at-history-of-presidents-meeting-the-pope

weaponry used to force people to get and keep their computer chips and mandated shots who would be the most upset. Remember those guys? Sorry, it's not them.

Nope. According to the scriptures, it's all of the sissy "merchants" who are crying over the fall of the Beast and its Whore. Merchants? Are you kidding me? I mean how maniacal and evil looking can Hollywood really make a guy who sells "cinnamon," "wine," "fine flour," "wheat," "Sheep," "horses," and all the "dainty and goodly" things like "fine" clothing and jewelry made of "gold, and silver, and precious stones, and of pearls" (vs.12,13)? Even Hollywood is going to have a tough time trying to make the guy who sells clothes, food and jewelry look really evil.

Here's a thought. Maybe, if we had just spent a little more time reading the scriptures and less time wasting all of our money on the things those merchants have been pushing on us – all of those fine goods that we have "lusted after" (v.14) – just maybe, we would have seen that the Beast actually creates an economic system that seduces everyone to buy into it with its paper dollar. It is an economic system upon which the Whore of Babylon is riding and being supported. Old Scratch most definitely pulled a fast one over on us.

I guess that's probably why he got the nickname the "old serpent." (Rev. 12:9) Like an old snake, he is so cunning that he actually "deceiveth the whole world" we are told. *Id.* He is the master of deception. He is the king of deceit. No one is any better at that sort of thing than him, and if he is going to get everyone to buy off on the Beast and his mark (aka currency), you can bet he is going to do it in a way that seduces and mesmerizes everyone into his game rather than forcing everyone into submission.

He would much rather have you do it willingly than to have to force you, don't you think? Seriously, if he gets you hooked on it, he's not going to have to keep wasting time trying to keep you on his side of the line. I mean, seriously, how many times has that tactic failed over the centuries? When everyone's being forced, there is always resistance, and the resistance always puts up a fight and always brings down the tyrants.

If he can just deceive and seduce everyone with his schemes, he doesn't have to worry about anyone fighting him on his plans to destroy the human soul. In fact, whenever anyone comes along, kind of like me, and tries to point out the scam he's running, strangely enough, the people will actually defend the scam and try and destroy anyone speaking against it.

Once people feel vested in the system, they can't bear the thought of losing it. The scripture tells us that he deceives "the WHOLE world." *Id.* (emphasis added) That's pretty compelling if you ask me. It's not a part or a portion. It's the WHOLE world – EVERYBODY. A dark, patently obvious evil and corrupt plan like the one Klaus Schwab is peddling isn't fooling very many people at all and certainly not the whole world.

Chapter 14
Another Beast Coming up Out of the Earth

"And I beheld another beast coming up out of the earth; and he had two horns like a lamb, and he spake as a dragon."
Revelation 13:11

As we wind down our discussion on the 7-Headed 10-Horned Beast, there are a few minor items that should be addressed before concluding. We know that the Mark of the Beast, as Delegate Read saw it, was the Beast's currency which we've demonstrated to be the U.S. paper dollar. We learned that the Framers rejected the proposal to give Congress the power to create the paper dollar in the Constitution but a corrupt and obviously compromised Supreme Court ignored the Constitution and destroyed it with its ruling in the *Knox* case.

In that case, the Court decreed that the Congress needed to be able to print paper money so as to avoid the dreaded "ruinous sacrifices." We learned that Washington is the man that John the Revelator saw on the Beast's paper currency, and that Washington's name is always associated with the letters DC, which translates into the Roman numeral six hundred – which was John's frame of reference – and that Washington left DC when he was sixty-six. We also learned that the paper dollar has been the world's reserve currency since WWII and, as such, all money on the face of the earth is controlled by the U.S. paper dollar – no one buys or sells without it. Bearing these things in mind, many of the remaining prophecies pertaining to the Beast are dealt with in this chapter.

For example, John tells us that everyone receives the "mark in their right hand, or in their foreheads." (Rev. 13:16) This is the verse that the one world government theorists hang their computer chip hats on. However, if we can just step back and calmly look at this prophecy in light of everything we've learned, we can see how it applies to the paper dollar. As with much of John's writings, this statement is pure symbolism. The right hand is Biblical symbolism that represents ownership, power or control by its possessor.[10] In other words, we receive the physical dollar with our right hand in a show of ownership.

Next, the mark in the forehead is also clearly symbolic and can be seen to represent the mind. John saw that the paper dollar would not only be used in its paper form but digitally as well. What better way to describe someone receiving a digital dollar than through the forehead or the mind? The digital dollar cannot be held except in one's mind. Thus, John saw people holding the paper dollar with their hands and the digital form of the paper dollar with their minds.

Another corresponding prophecy states that the Beast makes "war with the saints." (Rev. 13:7) Christians have been a target since Obama was in office, and the persecution has only increased in its intensity under the Biden regime, and I expect it to get worse.

Next, and this is where most one world government theorists base their entire thesis, John writes that "power was given him

---

[10] https://www.biblestudytools.com/dictionary/hand-right-hand/

(the Beast) over all kindreds, and tongues, and nations." (Rev. 13:7) Please note that it does not say the Beast destroys all nations, which is what would have to happen if we were to have a one world government, but the prophecy only says that the Beast has "power" over all nations.

By declaring that it only has power over all nations clearly implies that nations still exist. Otherwise, how else could the Beast have power over all nations? Under a one world government, there is only one nation – one government. While there are always nations who still try to defy the U.S., it is ludicrous to argue that it does not exercise worldwide power even over those nations who try to defy the U.S. The U.S. is clearly the dominant world power and exercises its power over all nations just as John describes.

Another prophecy of the Beast that we read about says that it has a "mouth speaking great things and blasphemies." (Rev. 13:5) This mouth, we learn, has power for forty-two months, which is 3.5 years. This is just six months shy of a full four-year presidential term.

I do not know as of this writing the identification of the "mouth," but I would suspect that someone like *Beijing Biden* could easily fit this description. It is no secret that he is unwell and seems unlikely to survive his full four-year term. He most definitely has no problem bragging about all the great things he has done, but any good Christian knows that he also blasphemes. He has wrested the scriptures time and again by coupling his abortion and homosexual/transgender talk with scripture. Pay attention to China Joe's ability to stay in office. I suspect he'll be gone by July 2024 – 6 months shy of his full four-year term.

Finally, we read about a second beast in verse 11. In that verse, John says he saw "another beast coming up out of the earth" with "two horns" and who speaks "as a dragon." I am also not as sure about this one and can only surmise what it means. Nonetheless, something coming up out of the earth can easily mean that this second beast will be made up of earthly materials.

Most likely, this second beast is a computer system that functions in two ways (i.e., two horns) and since John doesn't define these two horns like he does the ten horns, we can expect that it will keep within the traditional Biblical meaning of horn which is power.[11] One horn of power on this computer system is the ability to manage all things civilly through the internet (i.e., causing everyone to worship the 7-headed 10-horned Beast through tactics like censorship) while the other horn exercises power over all things militarily (i.e., doing great wonders like controlling missiles in order to call down fire from Heaven).

---

[11] https://www.biblestudytools.com/dictionary/horn/)

Chapter 15
The Beast and the Kings of the Earth

"And I saw the beast, and the kings of the earth, and their armies, gathered together to make war against him that sat on the horse, and against his army."
Revelation 19:19

When objectively considering the patterns of the past, one truth emerges to the devastation of everything else – the overwhelming majority of Christians will be like the Jews at the First Coming of Christ. They won't recognize Him or accept Him. Remember what the Preacher told us? *"That which hath been is now; and that which is to be hath already been; and God requireth that which is past."* (Eccl. 3:15)

The expression that "History repeats itself" is one of the major themes confirmed throughout the scriptures. The Prophet Hosea affirmed God's use of "similitudes" (Hosea 12:10). Without a doubt, He does not change but will keep using patterns to reveal Himself and His work to His children.

Patterns from the First Coming clearly intimate that the majority of Christians will in fact come to hate Him and want to kill Him when He comes the Second Time. The image of the Messiah that we have created in our minds, just like the Jews did, will not be the reality of who He is when He does arrive the Second Time. The Jews wanted a mighty Messiah of War but, instead, got the meek, mild sacrificial Lamb who atoned for the sins of all mankind. Am I right? Why would it be any different the Second Time around?

Today, we want the meek, mild, loving Lamb of God who forgives and loves everyone when He returns again. Our entire culture proves it. We hear it in all of the Christian songs and all the sermons. We see it in all the paintings and other art forms. Taken as a whole, they all depict a meek and mild sacrificial lamb of God. We even see it in many of the paintings that portray the Returning Messiah. He looks kind, loving and forgiving standing in the clouds surrounded by His angels. Yet, the prophecies found in the scriptures portray a much different image.

This is especially true in the prophecies concerning the encounters between the Beast and the Messiah. John says that, "I saw heaven opened, and behold a white horse; and he that sat upon him was called Faithful and True, and in righteousness he doth judge and *make war*." (Rev. 19:11) (emphasis added.)

Did you catch that? When He returns, He *makes war*. Do you realize what that entails? Notice also that John says that *he* saw "heaven opened." He does not say that anyone else saw "heaven opened" when the Messiah comes to make war. This point is critical as it means his arrival to "make war" is not something that will be broadcast to the world.

Remember when Christ first arrived in Bethlehem, the heavens were also opened, but it was just a few shepherds who actually witnessed that event. Everyone else living in and around Bethlehem and Jerusalem, at the time, was totally unaware of the meaning behind the Star of Bethlehem. Given God's proclivity for patterns, why would it be any different this time? If God is the same yesterday, today and forever and never changes, why would one expect that He is going to change things up at His Second Coming?

In light of these things, it is not unreasonable to conclude that when He comes again the Second Time, His initial appearance will not be announced to the world just like when He came the First Time. As best I can tell, the influencers have told their audiences that the Messiah will stun the world with an initial appearance in the skies for all to see. Yet, if we follow the patterns, only a handful will see Him initially, and fewer still will even be able to recognize Him in the beginning. The scriptures do say that He will reveal Himself, but it doesn't say when. However, if the patterns hold, it won't be until after He has been here for a while – most likely thirty years or so.

This pattern of lost discernment can also be seen in Christ's appearances after His resurrection. Remember all those people who had spent so much time with the Savior prior to the Crucifixion who were not able to recognize Him after the Resurrection? Mary thought He was the Gardener. John tells us that when she "saw Jesus standing" outside the sepulcher, she "knew not that it was Jesus." She even carried on a short conversation with Him before He called her by name, revealing Himself to her. (John 20:13-17)

Christ also spent quite a bit of time walking along the road to "a village called Emmaus" with two of His disciples asking questions and carrying on a conversation. Their "eyes were holden," however, "that they should not know him." (Luke 24:13-16) When they finally came to the village, "they constrained him" to come and "abide with" them for a while. Christ consented and went and "sat at meat with them." It wasn't until "he took bread, and blessed it, and brake, and gave to them" that "their eyes were opened, and they knew him" following which "he vanished out of their sight." (Luke 24:28-31)

Discernment was lost when Christ appeared to Peter and others while they were in their fishing boats. Christ was standing on the shore, we read, "But the disciples knew not that it was Jesus." (John 21:1-4) They had been fishing and had come up dry until Christ told them to cast their "net on the right side of the ship" and were unable to "draw it" into their boat when they did cast it "for the multitude of fishes" they caught. (John 21:6)

Realizing it had to be Christ because of their catch, the disciples hurried back to shore. Still, they didn't recognize Him as the scripture points out that "none of the disciples durst ask him, Who art thou?" since they already had figured it must be Him. How was it that no one actually recognized Him? (John 21:12) If the disciples, the ones who actually knew Him intimately, didn't even recognize Him, how does it make any sense at all that we will recognize Him when He comes the Second Time having never met Him at all?

It should also be pointed out that when Christ did appear at His First Coming, He didn't reveal Himself to His disciples. He asked them what they thought about His identity (see Matthew 16:13-18). He never actually revealed Himself to the religious Jews who were still professing their belief in the coming of the Messiah. As one who has studied patterns for many, many years, it makes sense, then, that Christ will not reveal Himself at first when He does arrive and will not be recognized by anyone when He does come. His revealing will come later.

This conclusion is supported by many of Christ's admonitions regarding His Second Coming. He tells us that He will come at a time when we least expect—"for in such an hour as ye think not the Son of man cometh." (Matthew 24:44) Why is this warning important? If nobody expects it, then how will they be able to even recognize Him?

The commandment to "watch" for the signs of His Coming are repeated over and over again in the New Testament ending with this—"If therefore thou shalt not watch, I will come on thee as a thief, and thou shalt not know what hour I will come upon thee."(Rev. 3:3) Why would it even be important to watch if we are all going to be able to recognize Him when He comes? Finally, it seems odd that He warns where not to look for Him— He won't be in the "desert" or in "the secret chambers" or other non-descript places. (Matthew 24:23-26)

He does tell us where to look thus indicating that it will take some discernment to be able to recognize Him. He specifically tells us to look to the "east" and to the "carcase" where the "eagles be gathered together." (Matthew 24:27-28) Why would these details be important if everybody will be able to recognize Him at His initial appearance?

There are other prophecies that help us with our discernment. As pointed out in the beginning of this chapter, the prophecy in Revelation Chapter 19 emphasizes the fact that when the Messiah arrives, He *"makes war."* The gravity of this prediction is lost on the influencers and, thereby, on their audiences. Those who have been talking about the Second Coming expect Him to appear almost magically in the skies, and then Boom! That's it! They clearly don't expect that the Messiah will first come down to earth and make war.

War is an ugly business because people always die in war. This fact alone means that people are going to have a difficult time recognizing Him let alone accepting Him. You know, just like the Jews did not recognize Him the first time because the Jews expected that He would come and start making war against their enemies. Today, very few will be able to see past the fact that their expected meek, mild, loving, and forgiving Messiah is actually the one who instigates war and wages it.

This spiritual myopia will be compounded by the fact that He will not look or act like the sort of Messiah they have envisioned in their minds either. We've all seen the pictures of the handsome, long-haired, bearded man in a flowing white robe and crimson sash. This description does not comport with Isaiah's portrayal. Isaiah clearly points out that "when we shall see him, there is no beauty that we should desire him." (Is. 53:2) This was the same problem that the Jews had with Christ. They hated him because he didn't fit the narrative. He was a "winebibber" (i.e., He drank too much). They hated Him because He cavorted with sinners. I believe we would call that hanging around with "the wrong crowd." Yes, yes, the Jews envisioned a much different Messiah than the One who actually showed up and, for the most part, they have never gotten past it. They wanted someone who was much more regal, polished, and sophisticated, who would only cavort with the "right kinds" of people.

Given the concept behind scriptural patterns, I'm certain that Christians are going to make these same kinds of mistakes. They want the loving, peaceful, forgiving, meek, and more "god-like" Messiah that they have created in their minds. Unfortunately, Isaiah shatters those delusions as he did for the Jews, who were just as clueless of Isaiah's prophecies as we are today. What? You thought that just saying the words "I believe" was enough, and Christ would just scoop you up into the Heavens, and you wouldn't have to worry about the hard stuff like trying to recognize Him?

When's the last time you read the verse in Matthew where it says, "Not everyone that saith unto me, Lord, Lord, shall enter into the kingdom of heaven." (Matt. 7:21) You need to put that thought right out of your head and focus on the commandment to "watch" in order to identify the returning Messiah so you don't try and kill Him just like the Jews did. Remember—watch and be ready.

As for the crimson sash around His waist, according to Isaiah, when Christ comes out of Edom and Bozrah, His garments will be covered in blood: "Who is this that cometh from Edom, with dyed garments from Bozrah... Wherefore art thou red in thine apparel, and thy garments like him that treadeth in the winefat? ...their blood shall be sprinkled upon my garments, and I will stain all my raiment." (Is. 63:1-3) It's not a sash – it's his entire robe that's covered with blood.

These questions are being asked in Isaiah's prophecy because no one recognizes the mannerisms of the blood-soaked individual coming from the East. In fact, Isaiah's bloody description of the Messiah is punctuated with the statement that Christ has had these bloody desires in His heart all along: "For the day of vengeance is in mine heart..." (Is. 63:4)

This is where the story starts to get even more interesting. According to the Book of Revelation, once the Messiah does begin to make war, it is none other than the Beast and his allies who rise up to oppose Him. You know, because they will see Him as a threat to their dominion powered by their paper money. They will most assuredly start to demonize their enemy, much like the Jews did, by using different labels, this time, such as thug and murderer. The name-calling, however, will eventually give way to their own lustful desires for war. In order to stop the Messiah, the Beast has to gather up his armies along with the kings of the earth and their armies to fight against this threat to their wardriven culture powered by paper money: "And I saw the beast, and the kings of the earth, and their armies, gathered together to make war against him that sat on the horse, and against his army." (Rev. 19:19)

Which kings of the earth, you might ask? Well, John explained who they were back in his discussion about the 7 headed and 10 horned kings, which we have identified as the G-7 and the G-10 nations—"And the ten horns which thou sawest are ten kings, which have received no kingdom as yet; but receive power as kings one hour with the beast. These have one mind, and shall give their power and strength unto the beast. These shall make war with the Lamb, and the Lamb shall overcome them." (Rev. 17:12-14)

Notice once again that there is no one world government being talked about in this scripture. The Beast is only the dominant power in this alliance as it still has to work to gather the other nations together with their armies in order to fight the Messiah and His armies. It is also interesting to note that these kings only have "power" for just "one hour with the beast." Peter tells us that "one day is with the Lord as a thousand years, and a thousand years as one day." (2 Peter 3:8) Since there are only twenty-four hours in a day, one hour in the Lord's time would be one thousand years divided by twenty-four which comes to 41.67 years or approximately forty-two years if we were to round up.

The G-7 was formed in 1976 when Canada joined the group of six bringing the number to seven. If these kingdoms are to only spend one hour with the Beast in the Lord's time, it would bring us somewhere around 2018. Trump was in office at that time and had put the skids on the war-making tendencies of that alliance. He also challenged the very utility of these groups, which is why he had to be removed from office.

Even though he was ousted in 2020, the damage was done. It is quite obvious that the financial power and control of the G-7 and the G-10 is crumbling. Banks are collapsing. Central banks are moving to consolidate while trying to move everyone toward a digital currency. The BRICS countries, headed by China, are also making a move to unseat the dollar as the reserve currency. It would appear that, just as John saw, the forty-two-year hour is up, and that the reign of the Beast and the G-7 and G-10 is fast coming to a close. This fact doesn't mean that the Beast and its G-7 and G-10 allies are not going down without one last war.

It is important to remember, according to John, that the Messiah is the one who makes war first, and then the Beast with the rest of its allies gather together to war against Him. If the Beast and its allies understood against whom they were waging war, perhaps they would have second thoughts about it. Obviously, they don't know His true identity, which is why they engage in war against the Messiah or perhaps they do know but they have given themselves over to evil so much so that they don't care because of their insatiable love for money. If this is the case, they must believe that they can actually beat Him in their war. Remember, the Jews fought against and killed the Messiah at His First Coming, so why wouldn't evil think that it could prevail once again?

On the whole, though, it seems rather apparent that no one will recognize the Messiah in this scenario, except for the few spiritually alert individuals who have been watching and studying the signs just like we saw with the First Coming. Don't forget, when Christ came the First time, He did not preach publicly that He was the Messiah. In fact, when His disciples finally came to the realization that He was the Messiah and acknowledged Him as such, He "charged... his disciples that they should tell no man that he was Jesus the Christ." (Mat. 16:20) Also, after His resurrection, He didn't show Himself but to certain groups of His disciples. It was not a world premier event.

Right about now, I would think that you would be asking yourself this question, "Is there anyone who has been making war of late who is opposed, hated, ridiculed, and vilified by the U.S. and its allies who are lining up to fight a war against that person?"

Chapter 16
A Lake of Fire Burning with Brimstone

"And the beast was taken, and...cast alive into a lake of fire burning with brimstone..."
Revelation 19:20

In case you haven't figured it out yet, there is an individual in the East who has been making war of late. This individual is most definitely hated and has been villainized by everyone here in the West. Now whether or not this individual is the one who makes war as prophesied by John in the Book of Revelation chapter 19 verse 11 remains to be seen, but there are a number of interesting parallels with prophecy that suggest it could be this individual.

As one might expect, the members of the media, the intelligence community, the establishment politicians in the United States and beyond have all attacked this individual relentlessly since President Trump came into office. Another interesting tidbit can be seen in the way the United States has, under the illegitimate administration of China Joe Biden, begun to bring his NATO allies and their armies together to fight this individual.

In spite of what many have said about this one individual (that he is a "thug," a "murderer," "the antichrist" – you name it), it is interesting to note that no one else in the entire world, except this one individual, has warned the West about their complete abandonment of their Christian heritage. In contrast, we see this man making efforts to preserve that heritage back home.

For example, the individual of whom I speak has signed a law that prohibits the public display of anything from the alphabet community. This individual has argued for protecting marriage in his constitution and condemning homosexual unions. In today's Western woke world, anyone who stands against the alphabet people are attacked as bigoted, violent Neanderthals. Perhaps you even agree with this assessment, so what's the big deal you ask? Well, let's go back in history to answer that question.

In Jerusalem, sometime around 30 A.D., Christ told His disciples what to look for at His Second Coming. Among a few other events, Christ told His disciples that they would *"see* the abomination of desolation, spoken of by Daniel the prophet" (Matt. 24:15) (emphasis added), when He comes again.

Now, before we begin our analysis of this verse, I'd like to point out the obvious in case you've missed it. The Lord is telling us to watch for a societal condition (i.e., "abomination") and not the end result ("desolation") that ensues from that societal condition. In other words, we can't watch for the result first, which is desolation, because it will be too late by then as it will consume us. We have to watch for the condition initially, which is "abomination" as it will bring the "desolation."

Now let's analyze that societal condition and try to understand what abomination Christ is talking about. Christ specifically mentions one of the Old Testament prophets (i.e., Daniel) as a clue. Too many people are confused by the word and think of it as one specific thing. However, the most pertinent verse for our discussion, I believe, can be found in chapter 9 verse 27 of the Book of Daniel, where we learn that abomination is written in the plural – "for the overspreading of abominations he shall make it desolate." Christ specifically referred us to the Book of Daniel to understand the "abomination of desolation." If Daniel warns of an "overspreading of abominations" that will make "desolate," then we should probably understand the distinction between the plural and the singular if we are to understand Christ's meaning.

Think of it this way—abomination and sin are related words, correct? If we were to reword the scripture in Matthew a bit and replace the word abomination with sin, you should be able to see what Christ was saying in Matthew. Since the two words are related, let's substitute one with the other for illumination – "the desolation of sin" is much like saying the "desolation of abomination" don't you agree? This small change, then, makes perfect sense with Daniel's reference to the plural.

For example, most would recognize that the word sin in this context would clearly include the plural. Yet, it does not have the extra "s" at the end, but we realize that sin can be used in the plural with or without the "s." If sin and abomination are synonymous, we can see then that the singular use of the word abomination as used in Matthew does not conflict with Daniel's use of the plural.

The Old Testament also reveals that these abominations are not crazy, out of this world, strange, or unheard of either like so many individuals are expecting. You know, like demons coming through a tear in the dimensional wall brought about by the proton collisions taking place with the large Hadron Collider particle accelerator at the CERN laboratory in Geneva. No, actually, the prophets of the Old Testament are warning us about the everyday variety of abominations with which we are all too familiar but their meaning has been obscured in the woke paradise of today. Ezekiel agrees.

In Chapter 33 of the Book of Ezekiel, we read, "Then shall they know that I am the Lord, when I have laid the land most desolate because of all their abominations which they have committed." (Ez. 33:29). It's very simple. We need to be watching for the overspreading of the kinds of abominations that resulted in desolation in the Old Testament times and what to do when we see them spreading across our own nation.

Simple, though it may be, if we are not watching for them, we will miss them entirely before the desolation actually does come. Christ didn't want His disciples to be overtaken unaware, which is why He spoke about it in chapter 24. So, let's take a look at the Old Testament to determine what abominations brought about desolation in those days.

Those abominations have been around for centuries, and they always bring death and destruction with them. For example – "for the overspreading of abominations he shall make it desolate." (Dan. 9:37); "Then shall they know that I am the Lord, when I have laid the land most desolate because of all their abominations which they have committed." (Ez. 33:29); "Therefore shall ye keep mine ordinance, that ye commit not any one of these abominable customs…" (Lev. 18:30); "Defile not ye yourselves in any of these things: for in all these **the nations are defiled** which I cast out before you: And the land is defiled." (Lev. 18:24-25.)

In fact, Moses explained that these abominations are so bad that even the land itself would not tolerate them: "Defile not ye yourselves in any of these things… therefore I do visit the iniquity thereof upon it, and the land itself vomiteth out her inhabitants." (Lev. 18:24-25)

Curious yet – I mean with respect to the abominations? What are they anyway, you might well be asking? They must really be way out there for the Lord to wipe everyone out living on the Land of Promise, right? Well, Moses lists the dreaded abominations in two chapters, 18 and 20, in the book of Leviticus. Take some time and read them for yourself, but for now, here is a summary of the abominations that bring desolation according to the Old Testament: (1) people began to "profane (God's) holy name" everywhere (verse 3); (2) people began killing their offspring (verses 2-4); (3) people are seduced by the magic art (verse 6); (4) people began to disrespect their parents (verse 9); (5) adultery is common place (verse 10); (6) incest and pedophilia is rampant (verse 11, 17, 20 and 21); (7) other sexual perversions like bestiality are also woven into society's fabric (verse 15); and, finally, (8) homosexuality is common and accepted. (verse 13).

Don't be fooled. Society may change their acceptance of such behavior, but God does not change as we've discussed previously. As such, realize that these eight kinds of behavior have been classified as abominations. We should also realize that these abominations only bring desolation today just as it did in Old Testament times.

Christ mentions these abominations in Matthew and tells us to watch for the abominations. If you aren't watching for it and are taking all your queues from the propaganda arm of the woke mob, then you're going to miss what Vladimir Putin can obviously see – that the West has lost its way and has abandoned its Christian roots.

We kill our offspring; we blaspheme God's name without skipping a beat in our conversations and entertainment venues. Satanism and the magic culture are prevalent everywhere. Sexual perversions have not only saturated our lives, but that lifestyle must be worshipped or the alphabet people will punish you, and you will find yourself cancelled, sued or arrested.

The bottom line here is that we are guilty as a nation of committing every single one of the abominations that the Old Testament Prophets warned would lead to desolation. The abominations that bring desolation have overspread our nation. Like it or not, it is a fact, and if you are watching as Christ told us to do, you will be able to see the abominations that bring desolation just as He predicted.

In my prior work, *Hypocritical Nation*, I presented evidence showing that the Hale-Bopp Comet which arrived in 1997 and seen by the entire world for eighteen months was the sign of the Coming of the Son of Man just as predicted in Matthew 24:30. I also illustrated the patterns between the Star of Bethlehem, which many experts claim was a comet that arrived in April – the same time Hale-Bopp reached its perihelion (the point where it was closest to the sun and at its brightest point) on April 1, 1997.

Vladimir Putin arrived in Moscow in 1996 as a virtual unknown, and in less than three years became President of Russia. How does that happen? How does an individual move to Russia in 1996 as an unknown and become president by 1999. It seems highly unlikely unless something more was at play. His arrival also happened at the same time Hale-Bopp was in the heavens heralding the Second Coming.[12]

Vladimir Putin is also known for his affinity for horses and has been photographed riding a white horse. If you are angered

---

[12] https://www.britannica.com/biography/Vladimir-Putin

and/or offended by my pointing out these corollaries, let me just say that I am not going to defend any of them. They are what they are, and as Madison says, "Facts are stubborn things; And whatever may be our wishes, our inclinations, or the dictates of our passion, they cannot alter the state of facts and evidence." It is up to you to decide for yourself what you want to see and what you choose to ignore.

Here's another important fact with respect to modern warfare. We have placed our destiny in the hands of other nations along with the Military Industrial Complex and the NATO Treaty, which is exactly what Washington warned against: "Why, by interweaving our destiny with that of any part of Europe, entangle our peace and prosperity in the toils of European ambition, rivalship, interest, humor or caprice?"[13] John warned us in this regard as well – "he that killeth with the sword must be killed with the sword." (Rev. 13:10) We took up the sword last century and started killing a bunch of people unconstitutionally, and we've never put it back down.

What? You disagree, and you're outraged because you think that we are "the good guys"? You believe that we were justified in waging those unconstitutional wars because we were only killing the bad guys? This kind of thinking doesn't really square with reality. For example, remember when Bush called for a new kind of war. He called for preemptive war, when he called for "preventive war," which was code for preemptive strikes against a declared enemy.[14]

Bush and his war minions declared the Cold War doctrine of "mutually assured destruction" to be outdated. So much for the

---

[13] Washington, Farewell Address, 38.
[14] https://www.globalissues.org/article/450/the-bush-doctrine-of-pre-emptive-strikes-a-global-pax-americana

moral justification that allowed for the killing of an enemy only when it is done in the defense of our lives, liberties and freedoms after we have been attacked. Once upon a time, we believed in the principle of self-defense and would never have sought to justify killing an enemy who had never attacked us. Remember those times? Well, now we believe that it is morally justified to go on the attack without any provocation. We have become the terrorists as illustrated most recently by Lyin' Biden, when he blew up the gas pipelines of another country without any provocation to the U.S.

There are some more interesting corollaries found in Chapter 24 of the Book of Matthew, where Christ details the signs that will take place at His Second Coming such as those found in verses 26 through 28. To the person who is seriously interested and tries to listen and watch carefully, these two verses are extremely important. Christ actually tells us where we can find Him at His Second Coming in those verses. He tells us where to look for Him and specifically where not to look for Him.

In verse 26, He says do not to go into "the desert" to look for Him. This warning basically excludes the entire Middle East. He then tells His disciples not to "believe" that He will be found "in the secret chamber" either. In other words, He will not be in hiding but will be living openly for all to see just like at His First Coming. To reiterate, Christ tells us not to look for Him coming out of the desert. If someone comes from a desert region and claims to be the Messiah, you can rest assured that individual is a fraud.

Also, we are supposed to be wary and not be fooled into thinking that He can be found in some secret hiding place. He will be out in the open for anyone to see, which implies that most will not be able to recognize Him. If Christ were initially going to make a Blockbuster appearance in the skies for everyone to see all at once, you know, just like He DIDN'T do at His First Coming, then why go into this detail telling us where to look and where not to look? It's because He is not going to proclaim His identity in the beginning just like He did not do the first time around.

This is why He provides the information found in the next verse, where He tells us exactly where to look for His initial appearance. He explained that He will be coming "out of the east." The East is a large area, but we do know that it most definitely does not include the West nor does it include the deserts of the Middle East.

Next, He explains that He will come like lightning that will "shine unto the west." He doesn't say He will be lightning. He simply says that He will come "like lightning" from the East and will shine unto the west. Someone in the East will shine across the world for all to see and will strike across the world causing great destruction just like with lightning.

How does Russia fit into this narrative? Well, to begin with, Russia is about as far East as one can get. It is most definitely considered to be an Eastern Empire. Right now, Putin is moving west toward Europe and threatening the U.S. with nuclear missiles, which would, of course, streak from the East across the sky to the West causing untold destruction.

Vladimir Putin came from the East to make war and is being vilified and demonized by the entire West in order to justify their collective and, at times, proxy war against Putin. In fact, Putin has been so villainized that no one is allowed to say a single positive word about him or even conduct an impartial interview with him by the establishment. If you do, Mitt Romney and all the others in the D.C. and NATO establishment will say you are guilty of treason.[15]

Yet, as noted, Putin is the only leader providing clarity on all of the heretofore abandoned Christian values of the West and our incorporation of all things abominable. We have seen the abominations that bring desolation spreading over our nation along with all the nations of the West. Putin even produced a Christmas video wherein a traditional Christian family was delivered as a present to a young man who had been trapped in the abomination of a homosexual union. [16]

Not surprising, this video was described by the Western media as "anti-west propaganda", "creepy", "cringe worthy", "heartless" and, of course, "homophobic."[17]

My how things have been turned upside down just as Isaiah predicted. (Is. 29:16) What was once considered completely antithetical to the values of the Christian West is now considered anti-West propaganda.

Finally, in verse 28, Christ gives us one final clue about His arrival. He tells us to look for the place where "the eagles be gathered together" for they will be where the "carcase is." Now, this is another one of those scriptures that has generated a lot of controversy and theorizing. However, it is important to bear in mind that this clue was given in conjunction with the prediction that Christ comes from the East. In other words, He will come from a place in the East where there is a "carcase" that "the

---

[15] https://twitter.com/MittRomney/status/1503113473819041796?ref_src=twsrc%5Etfw

[16] https://www.dailymail.co.uk/news/article-11566339/Santa-Putin-features-anti-West-propaganda-video-Russia.html

[17] https://www.sportskeeda.com/pop-culture/creepy-cringe-worthy-heartless-santa-putin-video-leaves-internet-appalled

eagles" will be "gathered together" around. As always, history is a good place to start, when trying to solve any good mystery.

The double-headed eagle has been Russia's official coat of arms as far back as the Third Century. Not surprisingly, this coat of arms was dropped during the Bolshevik Revolution and replaced with the hammer and sickle of communism. Seventy years later, however, after the death of the Soviet Union, the hammer and sickle died and was replaced with Russia's original coat of arms – the double-headed eagle where one looks east and the other west.

Now, a double-headed eagle crest can easily be seen as "eagles" in the plural form that Christ said would be "gathered together," since the crest shows them joined together. Therefore, it can logically be argued that, since the fall of the Soviet communist state, the eagles of the Russian crest are gathered together over the dead "carcase" of the Soviet Union. Specifically, Christ predicted that "where the carcase is, there will the eagles be gathered together." (Matt. 24:28) In other words, the eagles are gathered together on the double-headed Russian crest over the "carcase" of the dead Soviet Union.

Even if you disagree with my analysis, you should still ask yourself are you prepared to be wrong and allow the corrupt D.C. establishment to continue with their insanity over the Ukraine war? A war that I've shown is unconstitutional, corrupt, has no end in sight, could lead to WWIII, has already taken close to $200 billion dollars from U.S. taxpayers and more than 100,000 lives? Still not buying it?

All that's left then is to repeat the words of Gamaliel from the New Testament: "Take heed to yourselves what ye intend to do as touching these men... Refrain from these men, and let them alone: for if this counsel or this work be of men, it will come to nought. But if it be of God, ye cannot overthrow it; lest haply ye be found even to fight against God." (Acts 5:35, 38-39). We should all be so wise when it comes to Vladimir Putin.

Either way, Putin has issued a number of ominous warnings against the United States and its NATO allies for getting involved in the Ukraine war. Putin has also warned that Russia will utilize their nuclear arsenal against the United States and its NATO allies for their involvement in the war, which as I've pointed out correlates with the wisdom and advice of George Washington. If Putin uses nuclear weapons against the United States and its allies preemptively or defensively, the United States and its allies will burn with fire and brimstone. Once again this would be the fulfillment of another corresponding prophecy relating to the Beast which reads "And the beast was taken, and... cast alive into a lake of fire burning with brimstone." (Revelation 19:20)

Chapter 17
Should Be killed

*"And cause that as many as would not worship the image of the beast **should be killed**."*
Revelation 13:15

Now, I realize that this book has laid out some very unpopular ideas. I get it. The whole idea that the Messiah could come down without any fanfare only to wage war must seem so antithetical to mainstream Christianity that it's appalling. What makes it even more horrendous, I'm sure, is the fact that I actually suggest the Messiah might be the person from the East who has instigated an unprovoked war in the Ukraine. It's more deplorable because that person has been unanimously described as a "thug" and a "murderer." It just makes the blood boil – doesn't it? It's offensive on a primal level because if it were true, it means that the Messiah would be responsible for the destruction that comes with war including the killing of men, women and children. Most of all, the whole idea of it demeans the Messiah's regal, stately, image as a God in the eyes of everyone. Besides, it just doesn't square up with the Bible, right?

Well, now that you have brought it up, let's analyze it from a biblical point of view for just a minute. You know because the Bible should be considered our founding document as Christians. Surprisingly enough, almost right out of the gate, the Bible tells us that our God is "a man of war:" (Ex. 15:3) You probably didn't see that one coming. If He is a man of war, it is most definitely not a contradiction to say that, as a "man of war", He can come to "make war" (Rev. 19:11) just like John said He would. The Bible also tells us that He "will punish the world for their evil, and the wicked for their iniquity;" (Is. 13:6,9-11,19). Punishment? Now that's not a good word any more for sure. Most Christians today won't even touch that word, but there it is in our Bible. What's that you say? It's Old Testament stuff, and Christians today believe that their God is a loving God who forgives everyone and would never engage in the carnage of war? Well, then you're going to have to rip the Old Testament out of the Bible, because he doesn't stop there.

Isaiah also prophesied that "They come from a far country, from the end of heaven, ***even the Lord***, and ***the weapons of his indignation, to destroy the whole land***." (Is. 13:5) (emphasis added) Wow. Destruction of the entire land sounds pretty foreboding, don't you think? It doesn't stop there either. Jeremiah echoes this same sentiment. He says that the destruction from the Lord's weapons of indignation will cover the entire world: "And the ***slain of the Lord shall be at that day from one end of the earth even unto the other end*** of the earth;" (Jer. 25:33) (emphasis added) Notice it does not say the slain of a bad guy. It clearly says that it will be the "slain of the Lord." Isaiah continues with this same theme in another chapter: "For by fire and by ***his sword*** will the Lord plead with all flesh: ***and the slain of the Lord shall be many***." (Is. 66:16) (emphasis added) Isaiah doesn't stop, but keeps it going: "For, behold, the Lord will come with fire, and with his chariots like a whirlwind, to rend his anger with fury, and his rebuke with flames of fire." (Is.66:15) Look, I'm sorry to dwell on such dark things, but the Bible clearly shows that the Messiah is a man of war who will come to wage war as a punishment for wickedness, and that war will result in death and carnage worldwide. I'm sorry, but it's what the Bible tells us.

Keeping these facts in mind, let's turn our attention back to the United States and ask the same question. Are you appalled by the same aggressive war behavior of the United States or is it just the Messiah's aggressive behavior that offends you? Before you answer that question, let's look at some of the facts first. Since 1914, we have been leaving our shores to venture out and fight wars against numerous foreign nations, most of which we have instigated. Yet, the last time Congress officially declared war was on December 8, 1941 after we had been attacked by the Japanese. Every other war since that time has been instigated by the United States without a Declaration of War from the U.S. Congress. More importantly, every war since 1914 has been based upon a lie. Woodrow Wilson and FDR both campaigned on the lie that they absolutely would NOT send our boys overseas to fight a war in Europe. When in actual point of fact, they wanted us to get into those wars and were lying about it just to get elected. Surprised?

The Vietnam War was also based on the lie that our military forces had been attacked in the Tonkin Gulf and were not. The Iraq War was based upon the lie that Saddam Hussein was in possession of WMDs, which he was not. The twenty-year war in Afghanistan was based upon the lie that Osama Bin Laden orchestrated and directed the entire attack upon New York City with a cell phone, while hiding out in a cave in the mountains of Afghanistan. We all saw the controlled demolition collapse of Building 7. If you believe the official narrative, then it shouldn't come as a surprise as to why you fell for every other previous lie that got us into war.

Finally, take a look at the Ukraine War. It has been based entirely upon the lie that we need to protect the Ukraine in order to preserve democracy, when in fact, all of Zelensky's actions have been antithetical to a free society. Since the War, he has outlawed all of his opposition; he has jailed and assassinated his enemies; he has outlawed churches; and he has outlawed free speech, but just shut up about it, and remember that it has all been to preserve democracy. The real kicker about the Ukraine War is the fact that *China Joe "Pedo Pete" Biden* actually blew up Russia's Nord Stream pipeline even though Russia had not attacked us in any way, but MIC wants their regime change and by golly they're going to get it. You should realize that blowing up another country's pipeline without provocation fits the very definition of terrorism, correct? Terrorism is defined as the use of violence in the pursuit of political goals—the goal being regime change. Well, there you have it. Lies. Lies. Lies and more lies.

Now, what about our founding documents? How do those wars align with those important documents? What do they say about all of those wars where we were the aggressor? To begin with, Article I, §8, cl.11 of the U.S. Constitution exclusively places the power to declare war in the hands of the Congress and NOT in the President. Do you remember the reason for this? It's in the Declaration of Independence in case you forgot. It basically says that we didn't really like the way King George could move his military around the globe without any restrictions and engage in wars on a whim. Ring a bell? Now, it has been the U.S. president who has been moving his military around the globe without any restrictions in order instigate, declare, and wage war since 1941. These actions are in direct violation of the law laid down in our U.S. Constitution, and it sounds a lot like the president has been acting in the same manner as King George, don't you think? We also have the Great Rule that was laid down by the Father of our country, when he said that we are not to go abroad in search of monsters to destroy. From these descriptions, if you still think our wars have been legal and justified, it sounds like you know as much about our founding documents as you know about the Bible.

Let's see if I have this straight. You are still horrified by the possibility that the Messiah could come and start a war against a foreign country, which will result in death and destruction, even though the Bible not only sanctions such actions but it also prophesied that it will actually take place. Yet, in spite of your horror to the idea that the Messiah could do such things, you have never been horrified by all the wars that the U.S. has illegally, deceptively, and aggressively waged against other foreign nations – which have resulted in the killing and maiming of millions of men, women and children because, well, you are a Patriot, and you support our military... just not our U.S. Constitution, right?

Listen. If you believe in the Bible, then you believe that the Messiah is our God, which means He will always do what is right no matter how it may seem to us. The Bible also tells us that He is a God of truth and does not lie, so if He says that He is going to wage war when He comes again, as a Christian you are obligated to support Him in that war. On the other hand, the United States government is comprised entirely of humans who are NOT gods, and who also have a proven track record of habitually lying to the American people. In all seriousness, how can you support this kind of behavior, while at the same time condemning actions described by a God of truth? It all comes back to the patterns, I know. The Jews had their view of the Messiah, and we have ours – neither fit the correct view.

The Beast has done an amazing job at keeping everyone in awe and wonder of its image. The average American citizen doesn't even want to hear let alone believe that their government has instigated illegal and immoral wars that have resulted in the deaths of millions. Those same citizens, worse, still, refuse to see how paper money has been the engine running and powering all those wars. Additionally, no one will acknowledge the rampant fraud and abuse that exists behind the paper money scam even when some of it has been exposed. FTX anyone? Billions of dollars annually are laundered through corrupt foreign governments being classified as "foreign aid" and then back into the pockets of the politicians and their donors/backers.

It's insane how everyone worships at the church of the almighty paper dollar so willingly. Though, admittedly, some have tried to refuse and have had to pay the ultimate price. The unspoken rule is that no one can ever challenge or tarnish the impeccable image of the U.S. paper dollar. This means that the status of the dollar as the world's reserve currency can never be challenged in any way. As the scripture says, anyone who tries to undermine the image of our all-powerful economic system and what it represents will be killed—"...as many as would not worship the image of the beast should be killed." (Rev. 13:15). Here's another one of those corresponding prophecies that has to fit with the U.S. in order for it to remain consistent. Well, believe it or not, this sort of thing does happen, but there is always a cover story or, as some would say an "official narrative", that is used to deflect and obscure the truth. It should come as no surprise to learn that our corrupt politicians are capable of murder, especially when it comes to individuals or nations who try to break the monopoly that the paper dollar has as the world reserve currency.

Here's the hard cold truth. Whenever the all-powerful image of our financial system is challenged in the least, nations will be invaded, and people will be removed from power and murdered. Not buying it? Look, do you really believe that Hillary and Obama just wanted to invade Libya because it needed saving somehow even though it is far worse off now than it ever was under Gadhafi? If you remember from the video that made the rounds, Hillary was quoting Caesar when she said, "We came, we saw, he died… cackle cackle." Caesar's original quote ended with we conquered and not died, just so you know, and that is exactly what the U.S. did. It conquered Gadhafi and killed him for not worshipping the financial image of the U.S. Don't forget about Sadaam Hussein. Even though the media always reported those two stories one way, the deaths of Gadhafi and Hussein and the invasions of their countries were most definitely tied to their efforts to scrub the U.S. paper dollar.

Remember, the real story is always different from the official narrative. According to some observers, Gadhafi was trying to dump the U.S. banking system in favor of his gold Dinar and said that he wouldn't buy or sell any more with the paper dollar. He wanted to use his gold Dinar. You know because it was made out of gold.[18] Now you know the real reason he had to die.

Saddam Hussein was no different. He was also attempting similar efforts as Gadhafi, which meant that he had to die as well. When Hussein started to demand Euros for his oil instead of the

---

[18] https://thenewamerican.com/gadhafi-s-gold-money-plan-would-have-devastated-dollar/

paper dollar, it became a threat to the reign of the paper dollar and its all-powerful image.[19] Both of these assassinations and invasions were irresistible warnings to the leaders of other nations who definitely heard the message loud and clear, and it has kept them all in line for the most part.

Not everyone, however, has bent the knee to worship at the altar of the image of the almighty U.S. paper dollar. Putin is one such rebel. Putin has now tied the Ruble to gold. Do you remember from our discussions about how, prior to Bretton Woods, the use of the gold parity was a common practice by the world's powers in order to facilitate international trade payments? When Nixon took us off of the gold standard, every financial transaction became tied to the paper dollar instead of gold.

Besides tying his Ruble to gold, Putin has also announced that Russia will only accept Rubles in payment for European gas instead of our funny money just like we saw happen with Gadhafi and Hussein. As if to make matters worse, Putin has also indicated that the policy will eventually apply to all commodities and not just gas. The net effect of Putin's policy is, again, just like with Hussein and Gadhafi – to weaken the paper dollar's dominance as the global reserve currency. It should not be too difficult now to see why the U.S. has been trying to kill him and looking for a legitimate reason to invade Russia.

---

[19] https://www.counterpunch.org/2013/03/22/the-usa-attacked-iraq-because-saddam-had-wd/

Chapter 18
The Leaders of This People Cause Them to Err

"For the leaders of this people cause them to err; and they that are led of them are destroyed."
Isaiah 9:16

How does a nation like ours fall in such dramatic fashion? We were once a great nation uniquely blessed and protected by Heaven's invisible hand in our creation and our rise. Sadly, our corrupt leaders have led us down a path where we have discarded our Christian morals and the principles of our Constitutional Republic in exchange for the proverbial "bowl of lentils" baked over the dying coals of our current democratic system of government.

Evil, conspiring politicians have, over an extended period of time, changed our Republic into an unstable democracy that has become nothing more than a spectacle of "turbulence and contention" just as Madison warned in Letter 10 of The Federalist Papers. Very few people, if any, truly grasp or even understand this critical fact. All we ever hear from anyone these days is how important it is to "save our democracy."

Since we've destroyed our Constitutional Republic, the unaware majority have been flailing about inside our current turbulent and contentious political environment trying to hang on to anything of substance – not realizing that our political leaders and pundits have destroyed our Constitutional Republic.

Using the words of Madison, Hamilton and Jay from *The Federalist Papers*, I wrote *Spectacles of Turbulence and Contention*, to highlight how far we have strayed from the original structure of the Republic the Framers designed for us in our U.S. Constitution. According to Madison, our constitutional form of government was to be "strictly Republican" as "No other form," he explained, "Would be reconcilable with the genius of the people of America; (and) with the fundamental principles of the Revolution;" Madison, The Federalist Papers, Letter 39, 2.

To anyone watching the current political environment in the USA today, it becomes apparent that our Republic has been replaced with our contentious democratic spectacle. They can see this fact quite readily with the calls for defunding the police, labeling violent riots across our major cities as nothing more than legitimate "mostly peaceful protests", Congress spending us into oblivion, opening up and erasing our national borders, shutting down our energy industry, stealing elections in the open while denouncing those who call out the obvious cheating as crazy election deniers, destroying our Judeo-Christian heritage and our culture through child mutilations, drag queen performances in our schools and libraries, and on and on and on. We have truly devolved into the spectacle of turbulence and contention that is **democracy**, while embracing the evils of socialism and communism through tactics such as cancel culture, censorship, and poisonous mandates.

Besides highlighting the differences between republics and democracies, I also wrote *Spectacles of Turbulence and Contention* to warn of the catastrophes coming to this Nation due to our apostasy from the sacred law given to us in our U.S. Constitution and, yes, Madison himself argued that the Constitution was given to us by the "finger of the Almighty." Madison, The Federalist Papers, Ltr. 37, 15.

I wrote on the last page of *Spectacles* on June 23, 2019, that China would covertly attack the U.S. with a biological agent, beginning with New York City, within five years from my prediction—"I am confident that… the U.S. will see the destruction of several large American cities from either a nuclear terrorist attack or a biological attack or both within five years. Most likely the cities will include Los Angeles and New York."

I further explained that this attack would "be funded and coordinated indirectly by our modern-day Assyrian enemies (China/Russia)… They will also collude with several traitorous, large American corporations in order to fashion a false narrative…" The first attack came before the end of the year 2019 and Big Tech and the mainstream media have been completely complicit in fashioning the false narratives surrounding the attack and the false, poisonous remedies for it.

In my second book, *Hypocritical Nation*, that I wrote in 2020, I also predicted that the U.S. would face a Chinese invasion by or before 2025 following a series of severe cyber-attacks, an EMP, or both on our electrical grid and our infrastructure. The resulting pandemonium I predicted would set up a Trojan Horse invasion coming through Hawaii then through the West Coast to the East under the guise of a UN Blue Helmet humanitarian mission but that the CCP would be behind it. Couple this scenario now with the potential of the Russians attacking us from the East with their nuclear weapons, and it should be enough to motivate all of us back into the fold through repentance.

To anyone with eyes to see for themselves, it should be readily apparent from the recent spate of disasters we have been witnessing in our country that the war has already begun. Trains have been derailing spilling toxins into our ground, air and water. Over one hundred+ food plants have been attacked and burned to the ground in just the past year. Commercial chicken farms and cattle ranches have also been attacked and burned to the ground killing millions of chickens and thousands of heads of cattle. Supply chains have been disrupted. Energy prices have skyrocketed as our energy industry has been shut down. Chinese spy balloons and other equipment have traversed our skies. The flood of Fentanyl coming across our southern border is killing over one hundred thousand Americans 18-45 annually, and yes, it is the CCP who is behind the flow of that deadly drug. Finally, the CCP was involved with Big Pharma, our media and corrupt politicians who pushed a deadly, untested gene therapy shot onto the American people, who are now suffering the harmful and deadly side effects from that poison. It has been called a "bioweapon" by some experts.

Unfortunately, I fear that we are past feeling – having surrendered to the abominations that bring desolation so much so that we will not be able to wake up and see what should be obvious. Hopefully, I am wrong, and there is still a chance to avert the coming desolation. Unfortunately, if we look to the past, our demise will be easily recognizable in the patterns found in the desolation of the ancient nation of Israel.

The record describes it this way: "Then the king of Assyria came up throughout all the land and went up to Samaria [the capital of the nation of Israel], and besieged it three years. In the ninth year of Hoshea the king of Assyria took Samaria, and carried Israel away into Assyria… they rejected his statutes [much like we've rejected our Constitutional Republic and our Christian morals], and his covenant that he made with their fathers, and his testimonies which he testified against them; and they followed vanity, and became vain [you can see the parallels with this one, right?], and went after the heathen that were round about them [i.e., they formed alliances instead of relying on the Lord much like we've done in ignoring our Constitution and the Great Rule], whom the Lord had charged them, that they should not do like them. And they left all the commandments of the Lord their God [much like we have]… And they caused their sons and their daughters to pass through the fire [i.e., they slaughtered their children]…" (2 Kings 17:5-17)

In short, the nation of Israel was destroyed, and those who were not slaughtered by the Assyrians were deported into Assyria. There was one remaining tribe that did not get deported, however; it was the tribe of Judah, which was centered at Jerusalem—"Therefore the Lord was very angry with Israel, and removed them out of his sight; there was none left but the tribe of Judah only." (2 Kings 17:18) This one pattern should give some comfort to the true believers who belong to His Church.

They had been warned about this destruction when they first entered the promised land—"And ye shall not walk in the manners of the nation, which I cast out before you; for they committed all these [abominations of desolation], and therefore I abhorred them." (Lev. 20:23) This warning was so important that Moses made it twice in his record: "Defile not ye yourselves in any of these things: for in all these the nations are defiled which I cast out before you: And the land is defiled: therefore I do visit the iniquity thereof upon it, and the land itself vomiteth out her inhabitants." (Lev. 18:24-25) Tragically, the nation of Israel ignored the warnings and became the very thing they despised in the beginning.

Israel had come to reject God's laws and His warnings and decided to change God's laws in order to justify their immoral behavior to be consistent with their brand of justice—all at the behest of their leaders. (2 Kings 17:16) They sought for the things of the world by asking for a consolidated/centralized government much like we are doing, (1 Sam. 8:4-7) which only brought tyranny and misery. They also began slaughtering their own children and became infatuated with the art of magic. (2 Kings 17:17)

Israel actually became more corrupt, idolatrous, and lacking in moral clarity than the nations living in the land before Israel took it over. As reported in 2 Kings, the Israelites were "seduced... to do more evil than did the nations whom the Lord destroyed before the children of Israel" took over the Promised Land. (2 Kings 21:11)

How did Israel succumb to these abominations, you might ask? While it is true that, individually, we are responsible for our own actions, when the abominations form at the top, they will cascade down into the heart of the individual citizens. The prophet Isaiah explained it this way: "For the leaders of this people cause them to err; and they that are led of them are destroyed." (Is. 9:16)

This is quite the indictment, and it most definitely has significant ramifications for us today. It is not the working class that has driven our nation onto the low road of destruction. It began with those in charge. We need to wake up and realize that the problem began with our leaders, and anyone watching should be able to see that our leaders have been trying to destroy our nation from within for a long, long time. As we read in Proverbs,

"When the righteous are in authority, the people rejoice: but when the wicked beareth rule, the people mourn." (Proverbs 29:2)

Without a doubt, we have been walking the same path trod by the Nation of Israel. Who can seriously deny it? We slaughter our children in the womb, in our schools, and now we are confusing them and mutilating them in their confusion. We have become infatuated with the magic art and satanism in our entertainment. We have trashed our Constitution in favor of wanting to be like the rest of the World with their love of world government organizations like the UN, the WHO, and the WTO. We threw away our Republic in favor of democracy which only serves the interests of the winners and keeps the forty nine percent in bondage. We have fallen for demonic philosophies such as saving the planet instead of our babies.

There are at least three classes of leaders in this country – the ones in DC, the political influencers, and the ones in our churches. It is a fool's errand to believe that the leaders in DC will ever change and bring our country back from the brink of ruin. They were the ones who got us here in the first place. Like the Lord said, you simply cannot pour new wine into old bottles, for the status quo is only interested in maintaining the status quo and will kill and die in order to preserve it. You cannot change it by working within the system. If we are serious about taking back our country, we must come to grips with the undeniable truth that salvation will NOT be found in Washington, DC. This country's political class is way too corrupt and too far gone. You cannot fix it.

How do I know this to be true? I know it because it has never happened in all of history. The status quo only releases their grip of power when the people finally rise up and revolt. There is only one thing the corrupt establishment in DC loves and wants, and that is paper money. They do not love our country. They do not love the Lord Jesus Christ. They do not love the people of this once great country. They only love unlimited supplies of paper money. Remember, every act of evil can be traced back to the love of that pestilence.

Our conservative influencers are not much different. I know that you don't want to hear it, but it's true. They ask for money incessantly. Money, money and more money! Additionally, these leaders will attack and demean anyone who argues against following their losing democratic strategies. The system is not only rigged, but the "democracy" these conservative influencers/leaders promote is antithetical to **everything** the Framers gave us. Our influencers do not seem to understand this undeniable fact. They gave us a Republic **NOT** a democracy. We have bastardized our Republic into the democracy we now have starting with the 17th Amendment which made our Senators subject to the popular vote. The Framers knew what they were doing by giving that power originally to the State Legislatures.

Madison explained that it would keep power in the hands of the States and become a "double security" against encroachments from the national government. Madison, The Federalist Papers, Ltr. 51, 9. The Electors were also supposed to elect the president without any influence from the democratic majority in a popular vote, but we've destroyed that additional check against the national government as well with our democratically held presidential elections.

These two changes alone, and there are plenty of others, have completely eviscerated the power of the states along with their ability to act as a check on the national government and placed it into the hands of a small oligarchy that now runs the political parties. Political parties are now the power in this country and **NOT** the states. These two things alone will prevent anyone or anything from ever changing the status quo. I don't care how many times they tell you that "we can overwhelm the system" by turning out in droves to vote on election day or how they can beat the system playing by the other side's rules with ballot harvesting and mail-in voting – **it cannot be done**.

Remember this little mantra the next time you are tempted to participate in their unconstitutional democratic system – same systems, same people, same results. It is a fool's errand to attempt to change their system by participating in their system according to their rules. It will never change no matter what the conservative influencers tell you as they continue to ask you for more and more money to fund their campaigns, their conservative events and their legal fees. Don't fall for it. You do a great disservice to our Constitution and yourself when you participate in their unconstitutional democratic systems and processes.

Democracy is terrible for a number of reasons, foremost being that it never protects the forty nine percent minority especially given the fact that they can cheat so effectively now that the fifty one percent has been turned into the forty nine percent. Madison explained it best: "The countenance of the government may become more democratic, but the soul that animates it will be more oligarchic. The machine will be enlarged, but the fewer, and often the more secret, will be the springs by which its motions are directed." Madison, The Federalist Papers, Letter 58, 10.

The Framers told us plenty of times how to fix corruption, but we refuse to listen because our conservative influencers will call us names if we even think about it, and then they will kick us out of the club. Listen. Hamilton did not mince words. He told us that if "the representatives of the people betray their constituents, there is then no resource left but in the exertion of that original right of self-defense which is paramount to all positive forms of government... ***The citizens must rush tumultuously to arms, without concert, without system, without resource***; except in their courage and despair. The usurpers, clothed with the forms of legal authority, can too often crush the opposition in embryo." Hamilton, The Federalist Papers, Ltr. 28, 6. (emphasis added)

Your conservative influencers and leaders will never speak of such things because they are not really serious about change. They just want to keep milking the system – meaning you – for more and more money. If real change DID ever happen, it would mean that they couldn't ask for any more money. They don't want that to happen.

Anyway, it's all moot as it would appear that the people today lack the will to follow Hamilton's advice. Besides, the usurpers seem to be in complete control – think J6. Your conservative influencers are not going to save you. If you keep sending them money, then you deserve what you get. Jesus Christ and the wisdom of the Founders is **ALL** that will save our country now and nothing else.

The leaders of the American church are not much better. They have turned from our Christian heritage and became slaves to the abominations that bring desolation. In fact, I would argue that our country's biggest export today isn't the paper dollar. It's sodomy – an abomination that always brings desolation in the Bible – and that with the blessings of our church leaders. Not only have we embraced and submitted to this abomination, we persecute anyone who refuses to bow down to it or speak out against it.

With respect to this third group of leaders, it is also all about the money with them. Since LBJ's unconstitutional attack on the churches with his policy of granting tax breaks to the American churches as long as they stay out of politics, it has made the U.S. president the *de facto* head of our churches. The churches are so fearful of losing their tax-exempt status, (i.e., losing all that money to the government) that none of them will ever dare stand up to the political establishment in DC. This is the real reason we heard absolutely nothing but crickets from most of our church leaders during the "pandemic." They should have been the ones speaking out about the unconstitutional church closures and especially against the dangerous, experimental gene therapies that were being forced upon a trusting and unsuspecting populace through unconstitutional mandates, but our church leaders were all complicitly silent or acted as cheerleaders in the matter. They did not want to lose their tax-exempt status. Again, it is always about the money.

Isn't it interesting that paper money was viewed as a vile "pestilence" and a "wicked project" by the Framers and, yet, it has become one of our "greatest exports" according to some? Isn't it interesting that prophecy is never what the status quo expects? Don't you find that, at the very least, disconcerting? How many times do we hear conservatives laud the Founders? Yet, those same conservatives are just as selective in what they want to tout about the teachings of the Founders as the next guy. Otherwise, they would have spent the time learning and talking about the history of paper money as I have done in this work. Though, admittedly, if they had, I would venture to guess that they would still view the feelings of the Framers on this subject as either impractical, naïve, outdated, on the fringe, or just plain wrong... but only on this one thing because like any good conservative, they love everything else about the Founders.

Too many of us will continue to embrace and defend what was once considered a "wicked project" by the Framers, believing it to be ok because we're all the good guys around here, and we have figured out how to use that pesky "pestilence" the right way. Yet, given the fact that we can't seem to stop the orgy of spending in DC and the fact that we keep arguing for balanced budgets, it would seem to undermine those beliefs. I'm sure we will all still believe that such problems are only minor hiccups that will be remedied eventually by the "experts." In the meantime, shut up and enjoy the ride because... science. The Founders just didn't have the right tools, that's all. They weren't technologically advanced or smart enough.

Conservatives will, for the most part, continue to justify their positions on the matter by giving lip service to the fact that the Framers were still very intelligent; however, they were limited in their understanding and couldn't see far enough into the future when technology demanded the use of paper money and now digital. We've got it under control, though, so no need to worry! Besides, Delegate Read was probably one of the crazy ones, and we should just ignore him. He was a reactionary because paper money is great! It's worked great for us for over one hundred years. Well, as long as you don't count all of the horrible recessions, depressions, market crashes, hidden taxes (i.e. inflation), loss of personal wealth, runaway government spending, lack of government accountability, trillions and trillions of dollars spent on unconstitutional wars, all of the fraud, abuse and corruption that has come with it, not to mention the huge fact that it is entirely **unconstitutional**, but aside from all that, any good conservative will tell you that it really has been great! Do **NOT** believe any of it.

You need to have the strength to forget what all your leaders have been telling you. There is only one way to save our Republic from the desolation that is coming—one way and one way only. It's not going to be stopped by electing a bunch of "better" politicians in DC. It's not going to be stopped by submitting to the corruption, while praying for our leaders. What needs to happen is that the entire nation needs to repent of the abominations we are committing or accommodating. We need to return to Jesus Christ who is the God of this Land. We don't return just by saying His name and singing a lot of songs about His name. Like He himself said, "If ye love me, keep my commandments." (John 14:15) You have got to put some action behind your words.

"Remember therefore how thou hast received and heard, and hold fast, *and repent*. If therefore thou shalt not watch, I will come on thee as a thief, and thou shalt not know what hour I will come upon thee," (Rev. 3:3) (emphasis added) and destroy thee. Stop giving away your hard-earned money and start crying repentance to the people of this country before it's too late.